M000300970

Differentiating Instruction With Menus

Math

Differentiating Instruction With Menus

Math

Laurie E. Westphal

PRUFROCK PRESS INC.
WACO, TEXAS

Prufrock Press Inc.
P.O. Box 8813
Waco, TX 76714-8813
Phone: (800) 998-2208
Fax: (800) 240-0333
http://www.prufrock.com

For Ellen Williams, whose famous words kicked me into gear: "Start speaking more, publish a book, and go out on your own!"

CONTENTS

THE MENUS   49

CHAPTER 1

{ Choice }

"So, I can do as many as I want? Really?" stuttered one of my second-grade students as he looked, surprised, from the paper in his hand to me. I had just handed out a Getting to Know You List menu and explained to the small-group members that they would need to complete at least three choices from the list in order to share a few things about themselves with the group and me.

CHOICE IN THE PRIMARY GRADES

"I think it is the best one because I like it."
—*Kindergarten student, when asked to defend his activity of choice*

Choice can be frustrating for both the teacher who is trying to draw the best from his or her young students and the students who are trying to do what the teacher is asking, but are just not sure how to do it. Choice and independent thinking on a higher level are both developmental in nature, as well as cognitive skills. When given a choice between tools to complete a product, most primary students have not developed their higher level thinking skills enough to respond with a well-thought-out, analytical

1

response. Instead, a 5-year-old may defend or evaluate his choice by stating that it was the one he liked or that it was red, his favorite color. Does that imply that primary students are not capable of making choices or processing at the analysis level or higher? Definitely not! Primary students are very capable of making choices and enjoy doing so with some guidance. This guidance comes in minimizing the number of choices a student faces at once, as well as assisting in the choice process.

MAKING GOOD CHOICES IS A SKILL

"I wanted you to know, I never thought of it [making good choices as a skill] that way. That really opened my eyes."

—*Kindergarten teacher*

When we think of making a good choice as a skill, much like writing an effective paragraph, it becomes easy enough to understand the processes needed to encourage primary students to make their own choices. In keeping with this analogy, children could certainly figure out how to write on their own, perhaps even how to compose sentences and paragraphs by using other examples as models. Imagine, however, the progress and strength of the writing produced when children are given guidance and even the most basic of instruction on how to accomplish this task. The written piece is still their own, but the quality of the finished piece is much stronger when guidance is given during the process. The same is true with the quality of choices children can make in the classroom.

As with writing, primary students can make choices on their own, but when the teacher provides background knowledge and assistance, those choices become more meaningful, and the products become richer. Although all students certainly need guidance, primary students will need the most; they often have not been in an educational setting long enough to have experienced different products, and the idea of choice is usually new to them. Some children may have experienced choice only when their parents allowed them to choose between different outfits or breakfast options for the day. Some may not have experienced even this level of choice. This can cause frustration for both the teacher and the student.

> "When it comes to choice, some of my students just aren't receptive."
>
> *—First-grade teacher*

So, what is the best way to provide this guidance and develop students' skill of making good choices? First, choose the appropriate number of options for your students. Although the goal might be to have students choose between nine different options, teachers should start by having their students choose between three predetermined choices the first day. For example, if there are nine choices available on the menu, the teacher could break the menu into three different parts and allow students to choose between three of the options from the first part of the menu. Then, after those products have been created, students can choose between another set of three options a few days later, and perhaps another three the following week. By breaking down students' choices, teachers are reinforcing how to approach a more complex and/or varied choice format in the future. Primary students, even kindergarten students, can work up to making complex choices from longer lists of options as their choice skill level increases.

> "My first menu bombed. I had given it out to the students, told them to pick what they wanted to do, [and given them] the deadline at the end of the week. Students either bugged me all week with questions or they didn't do anything. . . . The second one went so much better. I did a build-up with lots of excitement and guidance for each choice. My students did a great job! Some even did more than the minimum!"
>
> *—Second-grade teacher*

Second, students will need guidance on how to select the options that are right for them. They may not automatically gravitate toward options without an exciting and detailed description of each choice. For the most part, primary students are still in the "pleasing the teacher" phase, which means when given a choice, they will usually choose what they think will make the teacher happy. This means that when the teacher discusses the different menu options, the teacher has to be equally as excited about all of them. The discussion of the different choices has to be animated and specific. For example, if the content is all very similar, the focus would be on the product: "If you want to do some singing, this one is for you!" or "If you want to write and draw, circle this one as a maybe!" Sometimes, choices may differ based on both content and product, in which case both can be pointed out to students to assist them in making good choices for themselves: "You have some different choices in our Earth science unit. If you want to do something with dinosaurs and drawing, circle this one as a maybe. If you are thinking you want to do something with collecting rocks, this one might be for you." Primary students, although egocentric in nature, have not yet pondered who they really are and often have trouble choosing between product types and content on their own. The more exposure they have to the processing the teacher demonstrates, the more skillful they become in making their own choices.

WHY IS CHOICE IMPORTANT?

Now that we have established that making good choices is a skill, and that skills need practice and experience to master, consider the simple concept of choices or options. Ask adults whether they would prefer to choose or be told what to do. Of course, they are going to say they would prefer to have a choice. Primary students have the same feelings.

> "Pick, pick, pick! Pick, I get to pick!"
> —*Second-grade student, singing as she skipped to the center designated for working on menu products*

One benefit of choice is its ability to meet the needs of so many different students and their learning styles. The Dunedin College of Education (Keen, 2001) conducted a research study on the preferred learning styles of 250 gifted students. Students were asked to rank different learning options. Of the 13 different options described to the students, only one option did not receive at least one negative response, and that was the option of having a choice. Although all students have different learning styles, choice is the one option that can meet everyone's needs. Unlike older elementary students, primary students have not been engaged in the learning process long enough to recognize their own strengths and weaknesses, as well as their learning styles; therefore, they need to be exposed to multiple options so they can begin to discover their preferences. By allowing choice, students are better able to narrow their options in the future and choose what best fits their learning preferences and educational needs.

> "I liked making the board game. Can I make one for my next menu too?"
>
> —*Second-grade student*

Another benefit of choice is a greater sense of independence for the students. What a powerful feeling! This independence looks different at each grade level in the primary grades. Once students understand it is about what they really want to produce, they will have the opportunity to design and create a product based on what they envision—what they really want to create. They will, however, still need some guidance and reassurance that their approach to a task is on the right track. Allowing students to show their learning by choosing the products they create helps develop independence at an early age.

> "I like getting to pick what I want."
>
> —*First-grade student*

Strengthened student focus on the required content is a third benefit of choice. When students have choices in the activities they wish to complete, they are more focused on the learning that leads to their chosen product. Students become excited when they learn information that can help them develop a product they would like to create. Students will pay close attention to instruction and have an immediate application for the knowledge being presented in class. Also, if students are focused, they are less likely to be off task during instruction.

Many a great educator has referred to the idea that the best learning takes place when students have a desire to learn. By incorporating different activities from which to choose, students stretch beyond what they already know, and teachers create a void that needs to be filled. This void leads to a desire to learn.

HOW CAN TEACHERS PROVIDE CHOICES?

> "I really had to limit my students' choices at first; they were completely overwhelmed. Now, they just jump right in. My last menu had more than 15 choices on it. I even had two students use the proposal form!"
>
> —*First-grade teacher*

When people go to a restaurant, the common goal is to find something on the menu to satisfy their hunger. Students come into our classrooms having a hunger as well—a hunger for learning. Choice menus are a way of allowing our students to choose how they would like to satisfy that hunger. At the very least, a menu is a list of choices that students use to choose an activity (or activities) they would like to complete to show what they have learned. At best, it is a complex system in which students earn points by making choices from different areas of study. Depending on the experience and comfort level of the students, the menus can also incorporate a free-choice option for those "picky eaters" who would like to place a special order to satisfy their learning hunger.

THREE-SHAPE MENU

"My students enjoy the Three-Shape menus. It is easy enough for me to break apart for them, and they understand the concept right away."

—*First-grade teacher*

Description

The Three-Shape menu (see Figure 1.1) is a basic menu with a total of nine predetermined choices for students. The choices are created at the various levels of Bloom's Revised taxonomy (Anderson & Krathwohl, 2001) and incorporate different learning styles. All products carry the same weight for grading and have similar expectations for completion time and effort.

Benefits

Flexibility. This menu can cover either one topic in depth or three different objectives. When this menu covers just one objective, students have the option of completing three products: one from each shape group.

Friendly design. Students quickly understand how to use this menu. It is easy to explain how to make the choices based on the various shapes, and the shapes can be used to visually separate expectations (e.g., circles one week, squares the next).

TITLE

Directions: Complete three activities, one from each shape group. Circle the shapes you might like to do. Color in the shapes as you complete them. All activities must be completed by _____.

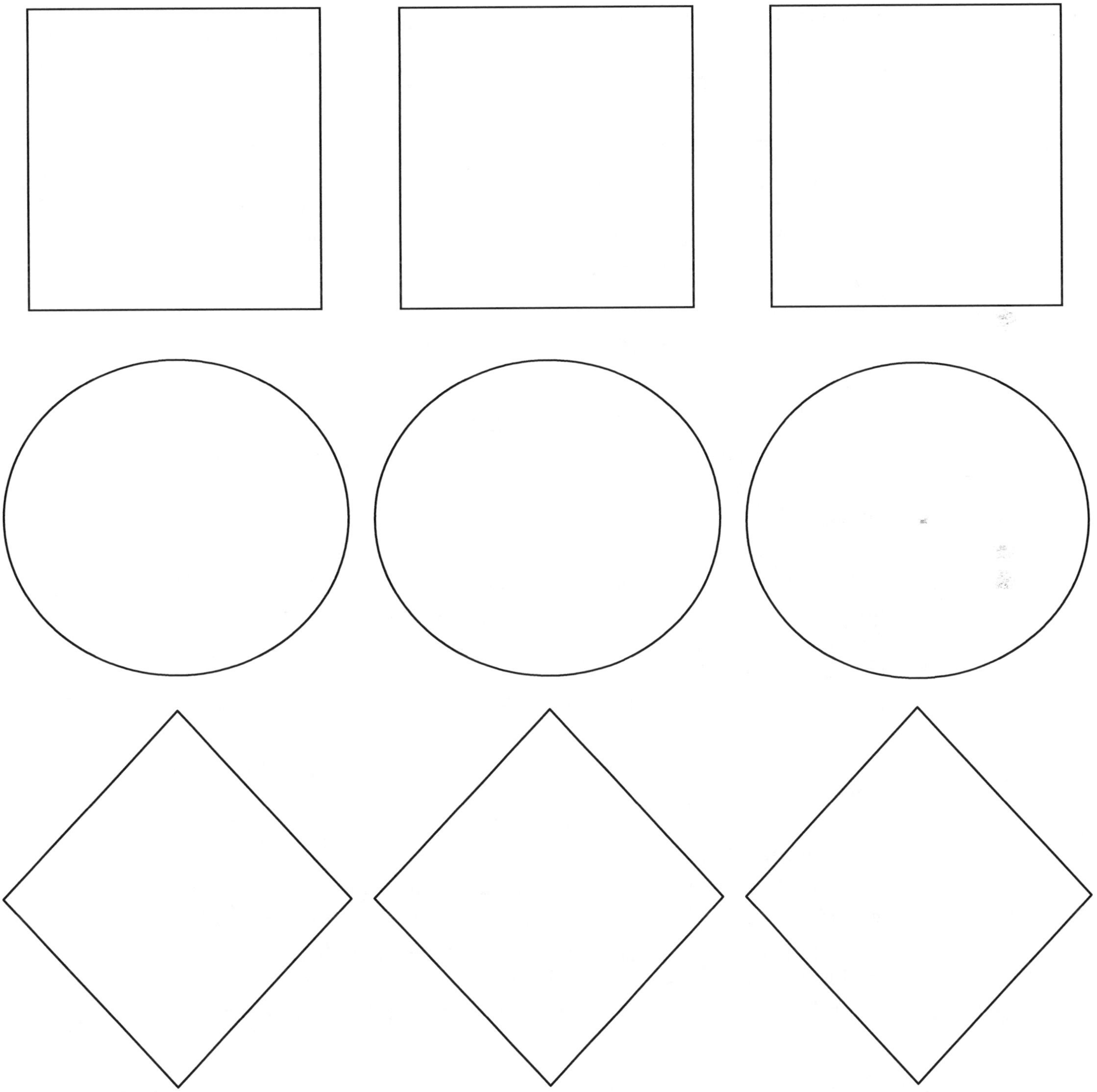

Figure 1.1. **Three-Shape menu example.**

Weighting. All products are equally weighted, so recording grades and maintaining paperwork are easily accomplished with this menu.

Short time period. They are intended for shorter periods of time, between 1–3 weeks.

Limitations

Few topics. These menus only cover one or three topics.

Time Considerations

These menus usually are intended for shorter periods of completion time—at most, they should take 3 weeks. If the menu focuses on one topic in depth, it can be completed in one week.

TIC-TAC-TOE MENU

"I like the tic-tac-toe one best because it was fun to do the different activities."
—*First-grade student*

Description

The Tic-Tac-Toe menu (see Figure 1.2) is a basic menu with a total of nine predetermined choices and possibly one free choice for students. Choices can be created at the same level of Bloom's Revised taxonomy or be arranged in a way to allow for the three different levels. All products carry the same weight for grading and have similar expectations for completion time and effort.

Benefits

Flexibility. This menu can cover either one topic in depth or three different objectives. When this menu covers just one objective, all at the same level of Bloom's Revised taxonomy, students have the option of completing three products in a tic-tac-toe pattern, or simply picking three from the menu. When it covers three objectives or multiple levels of Bloom's Revised taxonomy, students will need to complete a tic-tac-toe pattern

TITLE

Check the boxes you plan to complete. They should form a tic-tac-toe across or down. All products are due by: _____.

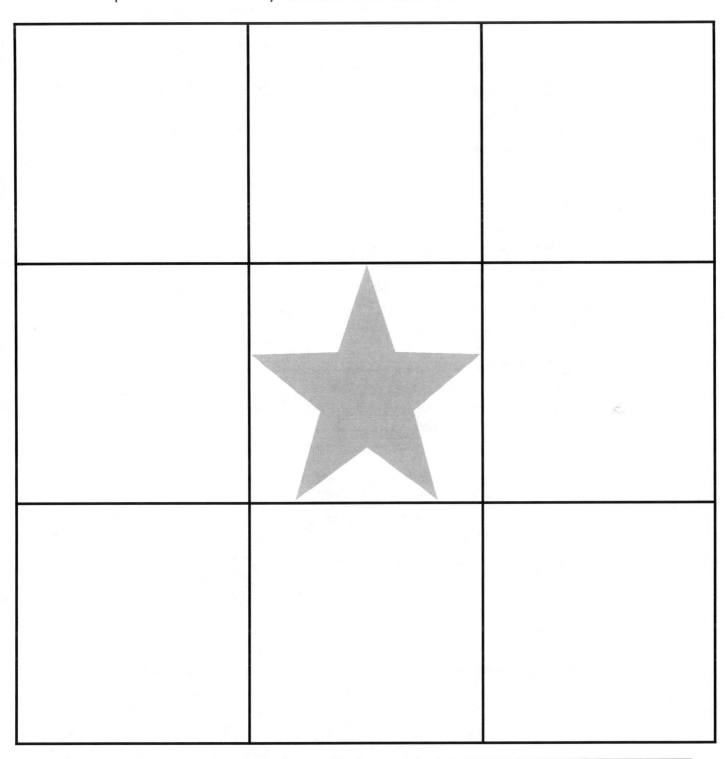

Figure 1.2. Tic-Tac-Toe menu example.

(one in each column or row) to be sure they have completed one activity from each objective.

Challenge level. When students make choices on this menu to complete a row or column, based on its design, they will usually face one choice that is out of their comfort zone, be it through its level of Bloom's Revised taxonomy, product learning style, or content. They will complete this "uncomfortable" choice because they want to do the other two options in that row or column.

Friendly design. Students quickly understand how to use this menu.

Weighting. All products are equally weighted, so recording grades and maintaining paperwork are easily accomplished with this menu.

Short time period. They are intended for shorter periods of time, between 1–3 weeks.

Limitations

Few topics. These menus only cover one or three topics.

Student compromise. Although this menu does allow choice, a student will sometimes have to compromise and complete an activity he or she would not have chosen because it completes the tic-tac-toe. (This is not always bad, though!)

Time Considerations

These menus usually are intended for shorter periods of completion time—at most, they should take 3 weeks, with one product submitted each week. If the menu focuses on one topic in depth, it can be completed in one week.

MEAL MENU

"I like choice. Can we do it again?"

—*First-grade student*

Description

The Meal menu (see Figure 1.3) is a menu with a total of at least nine predetermined choices as well as two enrichment options for students. The

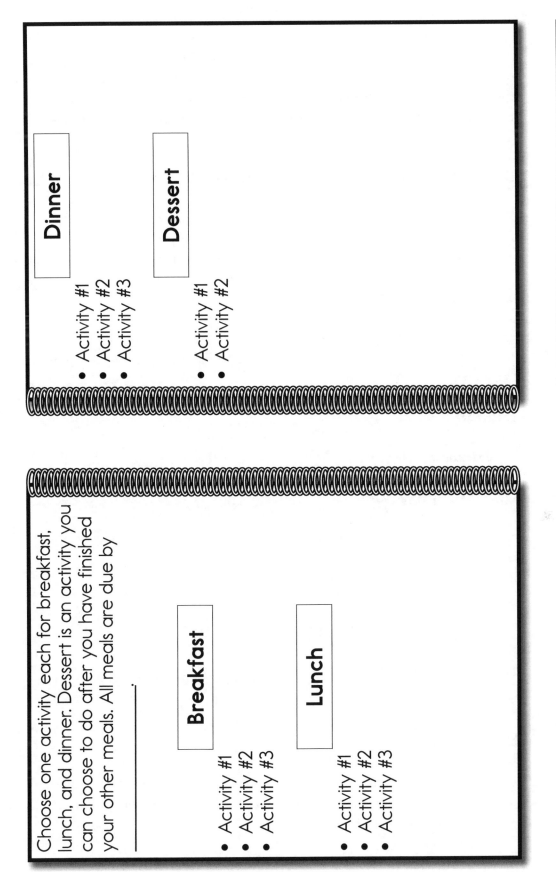

TITLE

Choose one activity each for breakfast, lunch, and dinner. Dessert is an activity you can choose to do after you have finished your other meals. All meals are due by ___

Breakfast
- Activity #1
- Activity #2
- Activity #3

Lunch
- Activity #1
- Activity #2
- Activity #3

Dinner
- Activity #1
- Activity #2
- Activity #3

Dessert
- Activity #1
- Activity #2

Figure 1.3. **Meal menu example.**

choices are created at the various levels of Bloom's Revised taxonomy and incorporate different learning styles. All products carry the same weight for grading and have similar expectations for completion time and effort. The enrichment options can be used for extra credit or replace another meal option at the teacher's discretion.

Benefits

Flexibility. This menu can cover either one topic in depth or three different objectives. When this menu covers just one objective, students have the option of completing three products: one from each meal.

Friendly design. Students quickly understand how to use this menu because of its real-world application.

Weighting. All products are equally weighted, so recording grades and maintaining paperwork are easily accomplished with this menu.

Short time period. They are intended for shorter periods of time, between 1–3 weeks.

Limitations

Few topics. These menus only cover one or three topics.

Time Considerations

These menus usually are intended for shorter periods of completion time—at most, they should take 3 weeks. If the menu focuses on one topic in depth, it can be completed in one week.

GIVE ME FIVE MENU

"The 5 menu was easy for me. I did my play and got 5 points!"

—*First-grade student*

Description

A Give Me Five menu (see Figure 1.4) has activities worth two, three, or five points. It is a shorter variation on the 2-5-8 menu (see p. 15), with

TITLE

Directions: Choose activities from the menu below. The activities must total 5. Place a check mark or color the picture next to each box to show which activities you will complete. All activities must be completed by

_____.

2

❑ Activity #1

❑ Activity #2

3

❑ Activity #1

❑ Activity #2

❑ Activity # 3

5

❑ Activity #1

❑ Activity #2

Figure 1.4. **Give Me Five menu example.**

a total of at least eight predetermined choices: at least two choices with a point value of two, at least two choices with a point value of three, and at least three choices with a point value of five. Choices are assigned these points based on the levels of Bloom's Revised taxonomy. Choices with a point value of two represent the *remember* and *understand* levels; choices with a point value of three represent the *apply* and *analyze* levels; and choices with a point value of five represent the *evaluate* and *create* levels. Each level of choices carries different weights and has different expectations for completion time and effort. Students are expected to earn five points for a 100%, and they choose what combination they would like to use to attain that point goal. As with the 2-5-8 menu, early primary teachers usually develop a way for students to understand their progress toward their point goals. Some will place boxes or graphics along the bottom of the menu so students can color in boxes as they complete different point values, and some will give pennies, tokens, or tickets as each product is completed so students can see the concrete results of their efforts.

Benefits

Responsibility. With this menu, students have complete control over their grades and/or how they reach their goals or target numbers.

Challenge level. This menu's design is set up in such a way that students must complete at least one activity at a higher level of Bloom's Revised taxonomy in order to reach their point goal.

Different ability level accommodations. Being point-based, this menu allows the teacher and students to contract for different point values based on modifications, time constraints, and abilities. For example, rather than five points, a student could be contracted for three or even eight as the target point value for 100%.

Limitations

One topic. Although this menu can be used for more than one topic, it works best with in-depth study of one topic.

No free choice. By nature, it also does not allow students to propose their own free-choice activity, because point values need to be assigned based on Bloom's Revised taxonomy.

Limited challenge level. Students will complete only one activity at a higher level of thinking.

Time Considerations

These menus usually are intended for shorter periods of completion time—at most, one week.

2-5-8 MENU

"It [2-5-8 menu] was fun. I got my 10 tickets and everything!"
—Kindergarten student

Description

A 2-5-8 menu (see Figure 1.5; Magner, 2000) has activities worth two, five, or eight points. It is a shorter variation on a longer, more complex List menu, with a total of at least eight predetermined choices: at least two choices with a point value of two, at least four choices with a point value of five, and at least two choices with a point value of eight. Choices are assigned these point values based on the levels of Bloom's Revised taxonomy. Choices with a point value of two represent the *remember* and *understand* levels; choices with a point value of five represent the *apply* and *analyze* levels; and choices with a point value of eight represent the *evaluate* and *create* levels. Each level of choices carries different weights and has different expectations for completion time and effort. Students are expected to earn 10 points for a 100%, and they choose what combination they would like to use to attain that point goal. Early primary teachers usually develop a way for students to understand their progress toward their point goal. As with the Give Me Five menu, some will place boxes or graphics along the bottom of the menu so students can color in boxes as they complete different point values, and some will give pennies, tokens, or tickets so students can see the concrete results of their efforts.

Benefits

Responsibility. With this menu, students have complete control over their grade and/or how they reach their goal or target number.

TITLE

Directions: Choose activities from the menu below. The activities must total 10 points. Place a check mark or color the picture next to each box to show which activities you will complete. All activities must be completed by

_____.

2 Points
❑
❑

5 Points
❑
❑
❑
❑

8 Points
❑
❑

Figure 1.5. **2-5-8 menu example.**

Challenge level. This menu's design is set up in such a way that students must complete at least one activity at a higher level of Bloom's Revised taxonomy in order to reach their point goal.

Different ability level accommodations. Being point-based, this menu allows the teacher and students to contract for different point values based on modifications, time constraints, and abilities. For example, rather than 10 points, a student could be contracted for 8 or even 13 as the target point value for a 100%.

Limitations

One topic. Although this menu can be used for more than one topic, it works best with in-depth study of one topic.

No free choice. By nature, the menu does not allow students to propose their own free choices, because point values need to be assigned based on Bloom's Revised taxonomy.

Limited challenge level. Students will complete only one activity at a higher level of thinking or, if contracted for other point values, could avoid the higher thinking options altogether.

Time Considerations

These menus usually are intended for shorter periods of completion time—at most, one week.

TARGET-BASED LIST MENU

"I thought it [List menu] looked really hard. There was [*sic*] lots [of activities], but then [my teacher] told me I only had to do 4 but I did 6. It was fun."

—*Second-grade student*

Description

The Target-Based List menu (see Figure 1.6) has a total of at least 10 predetermined choices and at least one free choice for students. Choices are listed in such a way that all of the options are similar levels of Bloom's

TITLE

Guidelines:
1. You may complete as many of the activities listed as you can within the time period.
2. You may choose any combination of activities. Your goal is to complete _____ activities.
3. You may be as creative as you like within the guidelines listed below.
4. You must share your plan with your teacher by _____.

Plan to Do	Activity to Complete	Completed
	Free choice—Submit a proposal form to your teacher for a product of your choice.	
	Total number of activities you are planning to complete:	Total number of activities completed:

I am planning to complete _____ activities.
Teacher's initials _____ Student's signature _____

Figure 1.6. **Target-Based List menu example.**

Revised taxonomy, in which the student is expected to complete a minimum number of activities.

Benefits

Weighting. All products are equally weighted, so recording grades and maintaining paperwork are easily accomplished with this menu.

Challenge level. When this menu is developed with multiple higher level activities, students must complete at least one activity at a higher level of Bloom's Revised taxonomy in order to reach their target goal.

Limitations

Few topics. This menu is best used for one topic in depth, although it can be used for up to three different topics, depending on its organization.

Cannot guarantee objectives. If the menu is used for three topics, it is possible for a student not to have to complete an activity for each objective, depending on the choices he or she makes.

Preparation. Teachers need to have all of the materials ready at the beginning of the unit for students to be able to choose any of the activities on the list, which requires advanced planning.

Time Considerations

These menus usually are intended for shorter periods of completion time—at most, 2 weeks.

POINT-BASED LIST MENU

"I like menus! I got to do a messy activity at the menu station cuz [*sic*] that is what I picked!"
—*First-grade student interviewed about using menus in his classroom*

Description

The Point-Based List menu (see Figure 1.7) has a total of at least 10 predetermined choices, each with a designated point value and at least one

TITLE

Guidelines:
1. You may complete as many of the activities listed as you can within the time period.
2. You may choose any combination of activities.
3. Your goal is 20 points.
4. You must show your plan to your teacher by _____.
5. Activities may be turned in at any time during the working time period. They will be graded and recorded on this sheet as you continue to work, so keep it safe!

Plan to Do	Activity to Complete	Point Value	Date Completed	Points Earned
		5		
		5		
		5		
		10		
		10		
		10		
		10		
		10		
		15		
		15		
	Free choice—Submit a proposal form to your teacher for a product of your choice.			
	Total number of points you are planning to earn:		**Total points earned:**	

I am planning to complete ____ activities that could earn up to a total of ____ points.

Teacher's initials _____ Student's signature _____

_____

Figure 1.7. **Point-Based List menu example.**

free choice for students. Choices are assigned points based on the levels of Bloom's Revised taxonomy. The choices carry different weights and have different expectations for completion time and effort. A point criterion is established that equals 100%, and students choose how they wish to attain that point goal.

Benefits

Responsibility. Students have complete control over their grades. Students really like the idea that they can guarantee their grade if they complete their required work. If they lose points on one of the chosen assignments, they can complete another to be sure they have met their point goal.

Concept reinforcement. This menu also allows for an in-depth study of material; however, if the menu uses the different levels of Bloom's Revised taxonomy, students who are still learning the concepts can choose some of the lower level point value projects to reinforce the basics before jumping into the higher level activities.

Limitations

Few topics. This menu is best used for one topic in depth, although it can be used for up to three different topics, depending on its organization.

Cannot guarantee objectives. If the menu is used for three topics, it is possible for a student not to have to complete an activity for each objective, depending on the choices he or she makes.

Preparation. Teachers need to have all materials ready at the beginning of the unit for students to be able to choose any of the activities on the list, which requires advanced planning.

Time Considerations

These menus usually are intended for shorter periods of completion time—at most, 2 weeks.

FREE CHOICE IN THE PRIMARY GRADES

> "I want to do an alphabet book. Is that OK?"
>
> —*Second-grade gifted student*

With most of these menus, students are allowed to submit a free choice for their teacher's consideration. Figure 1.8 shows two sample proposal forms that have been used successfully with gifted primary students. A copy of these forms should be given to each student when the menu is first introduced. The form used is based on the type of menu being presented. For example, if you are using the Tic-Tac-Toe menu, there is no need to submit a point proposal.

A discussion should be held with the students so they understand the expectations of a free choice. There are always a few students who do not want to complete a task on the menu or have their own idea of what they would like to do; they are welcome to create their own free choice and submit it for approval. The more free choice is used and encouraged, the more students will begin to request it. How the students show their knowledge will begin to shift from teacher-focused to student-designed activities. If students do not want to make a proposal using the proposal form after the teacher has discussed the entire menu and its activities, they can place the unused form in a designated place in the classroom. Others may want to use the form, and it is often surprising who wants to submit a proposal form after hearing about the opportunity.

Proposal forms must be submitted before students begin working on their free-choice products. The teacher then knows what the students are working on, and the students know the expectations the teacher has for their products. Once approved, the forms can be stapled to the students' menu sheets. The students can refer to their own form as they develop their free-choice product, and when the grading takes place, the teacher can refer to the agreement for the graded features of the product.

Each part of the proposal form is important and needs to be discussed with students.

Name/Teacher's Approval

The student will fill in his or her name. The student must submit this form to the teacher for approval. The teacher will carefully review all of

....

Name _____   Teacher's Approval: _____

FREE-CHOICE PROPOSAL FORM

1. What will you learn about? _____

_____

_____

2. What will it look like?_____

_____

_____

3. What will you need from the teacher to make it? _____

_____

Name _____   Teacher's Approval: _____

FREE-CHOICE PROPOSAL FORM FOR POINT-BASED MENU

I want to create something for _____ points. Points Approved: _____

1. What will you learn about? _____

_____

_____

2. What will it look like?_____

_____

_____

3. What will you need from the teacher to make it? _____

_____

_____

Figure 1.8. **Sample proposal forms for free choice.**

the information, send it back to the student for correction if needed, and then sign the top.

Points Requested

Found only on the proposal form for point-based menus, this is usually where negotiation needs to take place. Students will usually submit their first request for a very high number (often the 100% goal). They equate the amount of time something will take with the number of points to be earned. But please note that the points are *always* based on the levels of Bloom's Revised taxonomy. For example, a PowerPoint presentation with a vocabulary word quiz would get minimal points, although it may have taken a long time to create.

Points Approved

Found only on the proposal form for point-based menus, this is the final decision recorded by the teacher once the point haggling is finished.

Proposal Outline

This is where the student will describe the product he or she intends to complete. Primary students may need some assistance refining and narrowing their ideas. Teachers should ask questions to understand what students plan to complete, as well as to ensure student understanding. This also shows the teacher that the student knows what he or she is planning on completing.

What will you learn about? Students need to be specific here. It is not acceptable to write *science* or *reading*. This is where they look at the objectives of the product and choose which objective their product demonstrates.

What will it look like? It is important for this section to be as detailed as possible. If a student cannot express what the product will look like, he or she probably has not given the free-choice plan enough thought.

What will you need from the teacher to make it? This is an important consideration. Sometimes students do not have the means to purchase items for their product. This can be negotiated, but if teachers ask students to think about what they may need, they will often develop even grander ideas for their free choice.

CHAPTER 2

How to Use Menus in the Classroom

There are different ways to use instructional menus in the classroom. In order to decide how to implement each menu, the following should be considered: (a) how much prior knowledge of the topic being taught the students have before the unit or lesson begins, (b) how much information is readily available for students to obtain on their own, and (c) how self-reliant the students are when it comes to obtaining information. After considering these three items, there are four customary ways to use menus in the classroom.

ENRICHMENT AND SUPPLEMENTAL ACTIVITIES

Using the menus for enrichment and supplementary activities is the most common way to implement these tools. Teachers will often use their first menu in this manner, just to test the waters with their students. When using a menu in this way, the teacher will introduce the menu and the activities at the beginning of the unit. In this case, the students usually do not have a lot of background knowledge, and information about the topic may not be readily available to all students. The teacher will then progress through the curricular materials at his or her normal rate, periodically allowing class and homework time throughout the unit for students to work on their menu choices to supplement the lessons being taught. This method is very effective, as it builds in an immediate use for the content the teacher is covering. For example, at the beginning of a unit on animals, the teacher may introduce the menu with the explanation that students may not yet have enough knowledge to complete all of their choices. During the unit, however, more content will be provided and the students will be prepared to work on new choices. If students want to work ahead, they can certainly find the information on their own, but that is not required. Gifted students often see this as a challenge and will begin to investigate concepts mentioned in the menu before the teacher introduces them. This helps build an immense pool of background knowledge before the topic is even discussed in the classroom. As teachers, we fight the battle of having students read ahead or "come to class prepared to discuss." By introducing a menu at the beginning of a unit and allowing students to complete products as instruction progresses, we enable students to investigate the information and come to class prepared without making this a completely separate requirement.

COMPACTING SOLUTION

Given the task of compacting curricular units, teachers are often frustrated about locating alternative options to replace certain activities and lessons for those students who have "tested out." A common solution is setting up a preassessment with the stipulation that only if a student tests out of a unit completely will an alternate assignment be available, thereby decreasing the number of alternative options a teacher would need to find or create. The best model of compacting, however, allows students who show proficiency in just one piece or aspect of the unit of study to complete an alternate assignment. Menus can be used to serve this purpose; whether a student tests out of the entire unit or just one aspect, activities can be selected and offered to replace the standard instruction. If the entire class has access to the menu for enrichment, students whose curricula have been compacted may be contracted to choose between certain options to be completed instead of working on the planned curricular activities.

STANDARD ACTIVITIES

Another option for using menus in the classroom is to replace certain curricular activities the teacher uses to teach the specified content. In this case, the students may already have some limited background knowledge about the content, and information would be readily available for them in their classroom resources. The teacher would pick and choose which aspects of the content must be directly taught to the students and which could be appropriately learned and reinforced through product menus. The unit would then be designed using both formal instructional lessons and specific menu days where the students would use the menu to reinforce their prior knowledge. In order for this option to be effective, the teacher must feel very comfortable with the students' prior knowledge level. Another variation on this method is using the menus to drive center, or station, activities. Centers have many different functions in the classroom—most importantly, reinforcing the instruction that has taken place. Rather than having a set rotation for centers, the teacher could use the menu activities as enrichment or supplementary activities during center time for those students who need more than just reinforcement; centers could be set up with any materials students would need to complete various products.

MINI-LESSONS

The fourth option for menu use is the use of mini-lessons, with the menus driving the accompanying classroom activities. This method is best used when the majority of the students have prior knowledge about the topic. The teacher would design short 10–15-minute mini-lessons, where students would quickly review or introduce basic concepts already familiar to them. The students would then be turned loose to select an activity on the menu to show they understood the concept. It is important that the students have prior knowledge on the content, because the lesson cycle is cut very short in this use of menus. Using menus in this way does not allow the guided practice step of the lesson, as it is assumed the students already understand the information. The teacher is simply reviewing the information and then moving right to the higher levels of Bloom's Revised taxonomy by asking students to create a product. By using the menus in this way, the teacher avoids getting "I already know this," glossy-eyed looks from his or her students. Another important consideration is the independence level of the students. In order for this use of menus to be effective, students will need to be able to work independently for 10–20 minutes after the mini-lesson. Because interest is usually high in the product they have chosen, this is not a critical issue, but still one worth mentioning as teachers consider how they would like to use various menus in their classrooms. Menus can be used in many different ways; all are based on the knowledge and capabilities of the students working on them.

CHAPTER 3

Product Guidelines

"I just don't know what I want to do. Maybe something with markers."

—*Kindergarten student*

This chapter outlines the different types of products included in the featured menus, as well as the guidelines and expectations for each. It is very important that students know the expectations of a completed product when they choose to work on it. By discussing and demonstrating these expectations *before* students begin, and by having information readily available for students, teachers will limit frustration on everyone's part.

$1 CONTRACT

Consideration should be given to the cost of creating the products in any menu. The resources available to students vary within a classroom, and students should not be graded on the amount of materials they can purchase to make their products look better. These menus are designed to equalize the resources students have available. The materials for most products are available for less than a dollar and can usually be found in a teacher's classroom as part of the classroom supplies. If a product requires materials from the student, there is a $1 contract as part of the product criteria. This is a very important part of the explanation of the product. First of all, limiting the amount of money a child can spend creates an equal amount of resources for all students. Second, it actually encourages a more creative product. When students are limited by the amount of materials they can readily purchase, they often have to use materials from home in new and unique ways. Figure 3.1 is a sample $1 contract that has been used many times in my classroom for various products.

THE PRODUCTS

Table 3.1 contains a list of the products used in this book and additional products that can be used as free-choice ideas. These products were chosen for their flexibility in meeting learning styles, for their appropriateness for primary students, and for being products many teachers already encourage in their classrooms. They have been arranged by learning style—visual, kinesthetic, and auditory—and each menu has been designed to include products appropriate for all learning styles. Some products may be listed in more than one area, depending on how they are presented or implemented. The specific expectations for all of the products are presented in an easy-to-read card format with graphics that are very student friendly (see Figure 3.2).

The format is convenient for students to have in front of them when they work on their products. Each card has a graphic that illustrates most of the important criteria stated on the product card. These graphics are found on each menu next to task statements that require the corresponding product. This allows students to easily match a product with its criteria. These product cards can be cut out and put on rings for students to use as they work on their products. They also can be laminated and posted on a bulletin board or placed in centers for easy access during classroom work. Some teachers prefer to give only a few product guidelines at a time, while others will provide more cards so students feel comfortable venturing out in their free choices. The cards for the products mentioned in a specific menu can also be reduced in size and copied onto the back of that menu so they are available when students want to refer to them. Students enjoy looking at all of the different products, and they may get new ideas as they peruse the guidelines.

$1 CONTRACT

I did not spend more than $1.00 on my _____

_____   _____
                Student Signature   Date

My child, _____, did not spend more than $1.00 on the
product he or she created.

_____   _____
                Parent Signature   Date

Figure 3.1. **$1 contract.**

Table 3.1
PRODUCTS

Visual	Kinesthetic	Auditory
Acrostic	Board Game	Children's Book
Advertisement	Bulletin Board Display	Commercial
Book Cover	Class Game	Demonstration
Brochure/Pamphlet	Collection	News Report
Bulletin Board Display	Commercial	Play/Skit
Cartoon/Comic Strip	Concentration Cards	PowerPoint—Presentation
Children's Book	Demonstration	Presentation of Created
Collage	Diorama	Product
Crossword Puzzle	Flipbook	Puppet
Diary/Journal	Folded Quiz Book	Song/Rap
Drawing	Mobile	Speech
Essay/Research Report	Model	You Be the Person Presentation
Greeting Card	Mural	
Instruction Card	Play/Skit	
Letter	Product Cube	
List	Puppet	
Map		
Mind Map		
Newspaper Article		
Paragraph		
Picture Dictionary		
Poster		
PowerPoint—Stand Alone		
Scrapbook		
Story		
Trading Cards		
Venn Diagram		
Windowpane		

```
Write the word
Oval letters
Remember the word
Draw a picture
```

ACROSTIC

- Use a white piece of paper
- Must be neatly written or made on the computer
- Include the main word on the left-hand side
- Phrases must begin with one of the letters from the main word
- Phrases must be about the main word

Information

$8.00

Nice, White Shirt

ADVERTISEMENT

- Use a white piece of paper
- Color the picture of item or service
- Include price, if needed
- Can be made on the computer

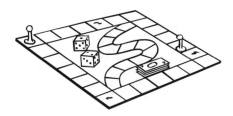

BOARD GAME

- Include at least four game pieces
- Include at least 25 colored squares
- Include at least 20 question cards
- Include the title of the game on the game board
- Provide written rules for the game
- Make board at least the size of a file folder

BOOK COVER

- Front cover—include title, author, and picture
- Cover inside flap—write a paragraph or sentences about the book
- Back inside flap—provide information about the author with at least five facts
- Back cover—tell whether you liked the book and why
- Spine—include title and author

Figure 3.2. Product guidelines.

BROCHURE/PAMPHLET

- Use a white piece of paper
- Fold the paper
- Include title and picture on the front page
- Provide at least five facts
- Can be created on the computer

BULLETIN BOARD DISPLAY

- Has to fit on a bulletin board or wall
- Include at least 10 facts
- Must have a title
- Needs to be creative

CARTOON/COMIC STRIP

- Use a white piece of paper
- Draw at least six cells
- Have characters talk to and interact with each other
- Use color

CHILDREN'S BOOK

- Needs a cover with the title and your name
- Must be at least 10 pages
- Include a picture on each page
- Should be neatly written or made on the computer

Figure 3.2. **Product guidelines.**

CLASS GAME

- Needs easy-to-understand rules
- Can be like a game you know how to play
- Should include questions for your classmates to answer

COLLAGE

- Use a white piece of paper
- Cut pictures neatly from magazines or newspapers
- Glue pictures neatly on the paper
- Label pictures

COLLECTION

- Have the number of items needed
- Fit items inside area
- Bring in a box or bag
- Include no living things

COMMERCIAL

- Should be 2–4 minutes in length
- Can be presented to classmates or recorded ahead of time
- Use props or costumes
- Can have more than one person in it

Figure 3.2. **Product guidelines.**

CONCENTRATION CARDS

- Make at least 20 index cards (10 matching sets)
- Use pictures, words, or both
- Write on only one side of each card
- Include an answer key that shows the matches
- Put cards in bag or envelope

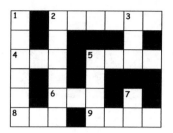

CROSSWORD PUZZLE

- Use at least 20 words
- Provide clues for each word
- Include puzzle and answer key
- Can be made on the computer

DEMONSTRATION

- Should be at least 2 minutes
- Show all important information
- Include two questions for classmates
- Be able to answer questions from classmates

DIARY/JOURNAL

- Should be neatly written or made on the computer
- Write at least one page for each day
- Include the date on each page
- Write as if you are the character

Figure 3.2. **Product guidelines.**

DIORAMA

- Use a box
- Glue pictures and information on the inside walls of box
- Write your name on the back
- Write information about the diorama on a card
- Fill out a $1 contract

DRAWING

- Use a white piece of paper
- Use colors
- Draw neatly
- Must have a title
- Write your name on the back

ESSAY/RESEARCH REPORT

- Should be neatly written or made on the computer
- Must include enough information about the topic
- Write the information in your own words (no copying from books or the Internet!)

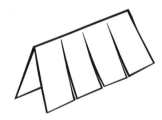

FLIPBOOK

- Use a white piece of paper folded in half
- Cut flaps into the top
- Use color for the drawings
- Write your name on the back

Figure 3.2. Product guidelines.

FOLDED QUIZ BOOK

- Use folded white paper
- Include at least 10 questions
- Write the questions on the outside flaps
- Write the answers inside each flap
- Write your name on the back

GREETING CARD

- Front—include colored pictures (words are optional)
- Front inside—include a personal note
- Back inside—include a greeting, saying, or poem
- Back outside—include your name and price of card

INSTRUCTION CARD

- Use heavy paper or a large index card
- Should be neatly written or made on the computer
- Use color for drawings
- Provide instructions

LETTER

- Should be neatly written or made on the computer
- Follow letter format
- Include all needed information

Figure 3.2. **Product guidelines.**

LIST

- Should be neatly written or made on the computer
- Include the number of items required
- Make as complete as possible
- Include words or phrases for each letter of alphabet except X for alphabet lists

MAP

- Use a white piece of paper
- Ensure information is correct and accurate
- Include at least 10 locations
- Include a compass rose, legend, scale, and key

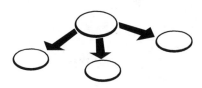

MIND MAP

- Use a white piece of unlined paper
- Must have one word in the middle
- Include no more than four words coming from any one word
- Should be neatly written or made using Inspiration Software

MOBILE

- Include at least 10 pieces of information
- Include color and pictures
- Include at least three layers of hanging information
- Ensure that it hangs straight

Figure 3.2. **Product guidelines.**

MODEL

- Should be at least 8" × 8" × 12"
- Label the parts of the model
- Include a title card
- Write your name on the model

MURAL

- Should be the size of a poster board or bigger
- Include at least five pieces of information
- Color the pictures on the mural
- May include words; must include a title
- Write your name on the back

NEWS REPORT

- Tell who, what, where, when, why, and how the event happened
- Can be presented to classmates or recorded ahead of time

NEWSPAPER ARTICLE

- Should describe what happened
- Design it to look like a newspaper article
- Include a picture to go with article
- Include all relevant information
- Should be neatly written or made on the computer

Figure 3.2. **Product guidelines.**

The sky is blue today.
I see a boat on the lake
and a man fishing. There
is a bird singing in the
tree outside my window.
I will soon eat breakfast
and go for a bike ride
with my friend Julie.

PARAGRAPH

- Should be neatly written or made on the computer
- Must have topic sentence, at least 3 supporting sentences or details, and a concluding sentence
- Must use vocabulary and punctuation

PICTURE DICTIONARY

- Should be neatly written or made on the computer
- Must have a clear picture for each word
- Draw or make pictures using the computer
- Use your own words for definitions

PLAY/SKIT

- Should be between 5–10 minutes in length
- Turn in written script before play is presented
- Present to classmates or record ahead of time
- Use props or costumes
- Can use more than one person in it

POSTER

- Use poster board
- Include at least five pieces of important information
- Must have a title
- Use both words and pictures
- Write your name on the back
- Include a bibliography as needed

Figure 3.2. Product guidelines.

POWERPOINT—PRESENTATION

- Include at least 10 slides and a title slide with your name
- Use color in slides and include no more than one picture per page
- Can use animation, but limit it
- Should be timed to flow with the oral presentation

POWERPOINT—STAND ALONE

- Include at least 10 slides and a title slide with your name
- Include no more than 10 words on each page
- Use color in slides and include no more than one picture per page
- Can use animation, but limit how much

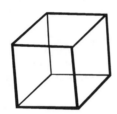

PRODUCT CUBE

- Use all six sides of the cube to provide information
- Should be neatly written or made on the computer
- Print your name neatly on the bottom of one of the sides
- Should be submitted flat (unfolded) for grading

PUPPET

- Should be handmade and have a moveable mouth
- List supplies used to make the puppet
- Sign a $1 contract
- If used in a play, all play criteria must be met as well

Figure 3.2. **Product guidelines.**

SCRAPBOOK

- Include a meaningful title and your name on the cover
- Should be at least five pages in length
- Include at least one picture on each page
- Include captions for all pictures

SONG/RAP

- Should be able to understand all words in the song/rap
- Can be a familiar tune
- Can be presented to classmates or recorded ahead of time
- Turn in written words
- Should be at least 2 minutes in length

SPEECH

- Should be at least 2 minutes in length
- Try not to read directly from the written paper
- Turn in the written speech before you speak
- Speak clearly and loudly

STORY

- Include all of the elements of a well-written story
- Should be long enough for the story to make sense
- Should be neatly written or made on the computer

Figure 3.2. Product guidelines.

TRADING CARDS

- Include at least 10 cards
- Should be at least 3" × 5"
- Include a colored picture on each card
- Include at least three facts about the subject on each card
- Can have information on both sides
- Turn in cards in a carrying bag

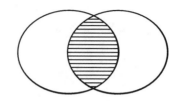

VENN DIAGRAM

- Use a piece of paper turned lengthwise
- Include a title at the top
- Include a title for each circle
- Should have at least six items in each part

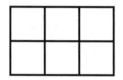

WINDOWPANE

- Use a white piece of paper
- Should be at least six squares
- Include a picture and words in each square
- Should be neatly written or made on the computer
- Be creative
- Write your name on the back

YOU BE THE PERSON PRESENTATION

- Pretend to be the person
- Include at least five facts about his or her life
- Present to classmates
- Should be 3–5 minutes in length
- Be able to answer questions about your character
- Use props or a costume

Figure 3.2. **Product guidelines.**

CHAPTER 4

Rubrics and Grading

"Rubrics are great for me, although my students don't always make the connection between the rubric and my expectations."

—First-grade teacher

The most common reason teachers feel uncomfortable with menus is their need for fair and equal grading. Teachers often feel it is easier to grade only one type of product made by all of the students, rather than grading a large number of different products, none of which looks like any other. The great equalizer for hundreds of different products is a generic rubric that can cover all the important qualities of an excellent product.

ALL-PURPOSE PRODUCT RUBRIC

When it comes to primary students and rubrics, it is often difficult to find a format that is effective to enhance students' products. The purpose of a rubric is to demonstrate for the students the criteria and expectations of the teacher, as well as to allow the teacher to quickly evaluate a product on these same criteria. When designing a rubric for primary students, it is important to look at what would be meaningful to the students. It should also be noted that many kindergarten and first-grade programs do not give formal grades for student work. This should be taken into account when using a rubric. Therefore, Figure 4.1 is an example of a rubric that has been classroom tested in the primary grades with various menus to encourage quality products. When number grades are assigned, this rubric can be used with any point value activity presented in a point-based menu. When a menu is presented to students, this rubric can be reproduced on the back of the menu with its guidelines or shared with the group along with examples. The first time students see this rubric, it should be explained in detail. This rubric was designed to be specific enough that students will know what criteria the teacher is seeking, but general enough that they can still be as creative as they like in the creation of their products. Because all of the point-based menus depend on points that are multiples of 5, the rubric itself has been divided into five areas to make objective grading easier.

Name:_____

ALL-PURPOSE PRODUCT RUBRIC

	Excellent	Good	Poor
Completeness Is everything included in the product?	All information needed is included.	Some important information is missing.	Most important information is missing.
Creativity Is the product original?	Information is creative. Graphics are original.	Information is creative. Graphics are not original or were found on the computer.	There is no evidence of new thoughts or perspectives in the product.
Correctness Is all the information included correct?	All information in the product is correct and accurate.		Any portion of the information presented is incorrect.
Appropriate Communication Is the information well communicated?	All information is neat, easy to read, and easy to understand if presented.	Most of the product is neat, easy to read, and easy to understand if presented.	The product is not neat or it is not easy to read.
Effort and Time Did student put significant effort into the product?	Effort is obvious.		The product does not show significant effort.

Figure 4.1. All-purpose product rubric.

The Menus

HOW TO USE THE MENU PAGES

Each menu in this section has:
- an introduction page for the teacher,
- the content menu,
- any specific guidelines, and
- specific activities mentioned in the menu.

INTRODUCTION PAGES

The introduction pages are meant to provide an overview of each menu. They are divided into five areas.

1. *Objectives Covered Through the Menu and Activities*. This area will list all of the objectives that the menu can address. Menus are arranged in such a way that if students complete the guidelines set forth in the instructions for the menu, all of these objectives will be covered.

2. *Materials Needed by Students for Completion.* For each menu, it is expected that the teacher will provide, or students will have access to, the following materials:
   - lined paper;
   - glue;
   - crayons, colored pencils, or markers; and
   - blank 8 ½" × 11" white paper.

   The introduction page also includes a list of additional materials that may be needed by students. Because students have the choice of which menu items they would like to complete, it is possible that the teacher will not need all of these materials for every student.

3. *Special Notes.* Some menus have special management issues or considerations. This section will share any tips to consider for a specific activity or product.

4. *Time Frame.* Each menu has its own ideal time frame based on its structure, but all menus work best with at least a one-week time frame. Menus that assess more objectives are better suited to time frames of more than 2 weeks. This section will give you an overview about the best time frame for completing the entire menu, as well as options for shorter time periods. If teachers do not have time to devote to an entire menu, they can certainly choose the 1–2-day option for any menu topic students are currently studying.

5. *Suggested Forms.* This section lists the rubrics that should be available for students as the menus are introduced. If a menu has a free-choice option, the appropriate proposal form will also be listed here.

CHAPTER 5

Numbers and Number Sense Menus

This page is intentionally left blank.
Differentiating Instruction With Menus: Math • Grades K–2

NUMBER WORDS
MEAL MENU

Objectives Covered Through This Menu and These Activities

- Students will connect number words, numbers, and graphical representations.
- Students will correctly use number words in different situations.

Materials Needed by Students for Completion

- Poster board or large white paper
- Blank index cards (for concentration cards)
- Large blank or lined index cards (for instruction cards)
- Ruler (for comic strips)
- Magazines (for collages)
- Materials for board games (folders, colored cards, etc.)

Time Frame

- 1–3 weeks—Students are given the menu as the unit is started. As the unit progresses throughout the week, students should refer back to the menu options associated with that content. The teacher will go over all of the options for that content and have students color or circle the graphic for each option that represents the activity they are most interested in completing. As teaching continues over the next 2–3 weeks, the activities chosen and completed should create a full day's meal, with a breakfast, a lunch, a dinner, and an optional dessert. The teacher may choose to dedicate a learning center to working on menu products or simply allow time to work after other work is finished. When students complete the menu with this expectation, they have completed one activity from each content area, learning style, or level of Bloom's Revised taxonomy, depending on the design of the menu.
- 1–2 days—The teacher chooses an activity or product from an objective to use with the entire class during that lesson time.

Suggested Forms

- All-purpose rubric
- Free-choice proposal form if appropriate for content and level of students

Number Words

Choose one activity each for breakfast, lunch, and dinner. Dessert is an activity you can choose to do after you have finished your other meals. All meals are due by _____.

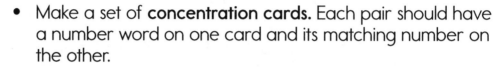

Breakfast

- Make a set of **concentration cards.** Each pair should have a number word on one card and its matching number on the other.

- Which number word has the most letters? Make a **list** of numbers and number words you think are long until you find the longest one!

- Create an **instruction card** for writing number words that are above 20. Give lots of examples.

Lunch

- When do people need to use number words rather than just write the number? Ask your friends and family when they use number words and develop a **comic strip** that shows one of these uses.

- Design a **collage** of number words that are found in magazines. Write how each number word was used.

- People sometimes use number words to show their addresses on their houses. **Draw** a picture of your house, and use number words to show the numbers in your address.

Name: _____

Dinner

- Write a **children's book** about animals that helps others learn their number words. Use numbers, words, and pictures!

- Create a **board game** that has players practice their number words.

- Develop a **class game** in which your classmates have to guess a number based on clues about the number word.

Dessert

- Number words follow a pattern once you get past 12. Why do you think this is? Does it happen in other languages as well? Research numbers in other languages and **report** what you find.

PLACE VALUE
2-5-8 MENU

Objectives Covered Through This Menu and These Activities

- Students will demonstrate understanding of place value.
- Students will locate and designate place values in numbers.

Materials Needed by Students for Completion

- Base ten blocks
- Blank index cards (for trading cards)
- Magazines (for collages)
- Poster board or large white paper
- Materials for bulletin board displays

Special Notes on the Use of This Menu

- This menu allows students to create a bulletin board display. Some classrooms may have only one bulletin board, so the teacher can divide the board into sections, or additional classroom wall or hall space can be sectioned off for the creation of these displays. Students can plan their displays based on the amount of space they are assigned.

Time Frame

- 1–2 weeks—Students are given the menu as the unit is started, and the teacher discusses all of the product options on the menu. As the different options are discussed, students color or circle the graphic for each option that represents the activity they are most interested in completing so they meet their goal of 10 points. As students complete products, they will color corresponding graphics along the bottom of the menu so they can track their progress toward their 10-point goal. As the lessons progress through the week(s), the teacher and students refer back to the menu options associated with the content being taught.
- 1–2 days—The teacher chooses an activity or product from the menu to use with the entire class.

Suggested Forms

- All-purpose rubric
- Free-choice proposal form if appropriate for content and level of students

Name:_____

PLACE VALUE

Directions: Choose activities from the menu below. The activities must total 10 points. Place a check mark or color the picture next to each box to show which activities you will complete. Color the circles along the bottom as you complete your activities to reach 10! All activities must be completed by

_____.

2 POINTS

❏ Make a **mobile** for a three-digit number. Tell the number's place value and draw a picture using base ten blocks to show the value of each digit in the number.

❏ Create a set of **trading cards** for five different place values.

5 POINTS

❏ Create an **advertisement** for a product that has three different place values in its price. Write the number and its values on the back of your advertisement.

❏ Make a **collage** of numbers and prices found in the Sunday advertisements. Label the different place values in each number or price.

❏ The ones place has decided it doesn't want to be a place value anymore. Write a **newspaper article** about how the 10s and 100s feel about this change.

❏ **Free choice**—Submit a proposal form to your teacher for a product of your choice.

8 POINTS

❏ Investigate either the Egyptian or the Roman method of recording numbers. Create a **brochure** that shows how their number system and place values are different than ours.

❏ One of your friends thinks that zeros are very important when it comes to place value. Make a **bulletin board display** that proves whether or not they are important.

◯ ◯ ◯ ◯ ◯ ◯ ◯ ◯ ◯ ◯

SKIP COUNTING
GIVE ME FIVE MENU

Objectives Covered Through This Menu and These Activities
- Students will practice various forms of skip counting.

Materials Needed by Students for Completion
- Poster board or large white paper
- Large blank or lined index cards (for instruction cards)
- Materials for bulletin board displays

Special Notes on the Use of This Menu
- This menu allows students to create a bulletin board display. Some classrooms may have only one bulletin board, so the teacher can divide the board into sections, or additional classroom wall or hall space can be sectioned off for the creation of these displays. Students can plan their displays based on the amount of space they are assigned.

Time Frame
- 1 week—Students are given the menu as the unit is started, and the teacher discusses all of the product options on the menu. As the different options are discussed, students will color or circle the graphic for each option that represents the activity they are most interested in completing based on a goal of five points. In this menu, that would imply students complete either two products (a two-point and a three-point) or one five-point product. As students complete products, they will color corresponding graphics along the bottom of the menu so they can track their progress toward their five-point goal. As the lessons progress throughout the week, the teacher and students refer back to the menu options associated with the content being taught. The teacher may choose to dedicate a learning center to working on menu products or simply allow time to work after other work is finished.
- 1–2 days—The teacher chooses an activity or product from the menu to use with the entire class.

Suggested Forms
- All-purpose rubric
- Free-choice proposal form if appropriate for content and level of students

Name:_____

SKIP COUNTING

Directions: Choose activities from the menu below. The activities must total 5. Place a check mark or color the picture next to each box to show which activities you will complete. Color the numbers along the bottom as you complete your activities to reach 5! All activities must be completed by

_____.

2

❏ Create an **instruction card** that shows how to count by 2's and 5's without using manipulatives.

❏ **Free choice**—Submit a proposal form to your teacher for a product of your choice.

3

❏ Make up a **class game** that lets your classmates practice their counting by 2's, 5's, and 10's.

❏ Create a **bulletin board display** that shows the patterns found in skip counting.

5

❏ You are a person who only likes even numbers and even-numbered things. Perform a **play** that shows all of the things you would not be able to do because you are picky about your numbers!

❏ Make a **children's** dot-to-dot **book** that uses skip counting to make at least eight drawings. Use different kinds of skip counting, and include an answer key in your book.

1 2 3 4 5

MATHEMATICAL SYMBOLS 2-5-8 MENU

Objectives Covered Through This Menu and These Activities
- Students will correctly identify different mathematical symbols.
- Students will be able to correctly use different mathematical symbols.

Materials Needed by Students for Completion
- Poster board or large white paper
- Socks (for puppets)
- Paper bags (for puppets)
- Recycled materials (for puppets)
- Coat hangers (for mobiles)
- String (for mobiles)
- Blank index cards (for mobiles and trading cards)

Special Notes on the Use of This Menu
- This menu asks students to use recycled materials. This does not mean only plastic and paper; instead, students should focus on using materials in new ways. It works well if a box is started for "recycled" contributions at the beginning of the school year. That way, students always have access to these types of materials.

Time Frame
- 1–2 weeks—Students are given the menu as the unit is started, and the teacher discusses all of the product options on the menu. As the different options are discussed, students color or circle the graphic for each option that represents the activity they are most interested in completing so they meet their goal of 10 points. As students complete products, they will color corresponding graphics along the bottom of the menu so they can track their progress toward their 10-point goal. As the lessons progress through the week(s), the teacher and students refer back to the menu options associated with the content being taught.
- 1–2 days—The teacher chooses an activity or product from the menu to use with the entire class.

Suggested Forms

- All-purpose rubric
- Free-choice proposal form if appropriate for content and level of students

Name:_____

MATHEMATICAL SYMBOLS

Directions: Choose activities from the menu below. The activities must total 10 points. Place a check mark or color the picture next to each box to show which activities you will complete. Color the addition signs along the bottom as you complete your activities to reach 10! All activities must be completed by _____.

2 POINTS

❏ Make a **mobile** of the mathematical symbols with an example of how to use each.

❏ Create a set of **trading cards** for the mathematical symbols listed above. Your cards should include examples of how each symbol is used.

5 POINTS

❏ Create a **picture dictionary** for the mathematical symbols. Be sure to include examples.

❏ Create a **brochure** that shows examples of the mathematical symbols and their proper use.

❏ Make a **play** that shows how important it is to choose the correct mathematical symbol. Include examples of how changing the symbol can have disastrous effects.

❏ **Free choice**—Submit a proposal form to your teacher for a product of your choice.

8 POINTS

❏ The addition sign has decided it is the most important mathematical symbol. Perform a **news report** about why addition thinks it is important and how the other mathematical symbols feel about this.

❏ Create a **puppet** for your favorite mathematical symbol using recycled materials. Perform a puppet show where your symbol talks about why it is the best symbol and what it does to numbers.

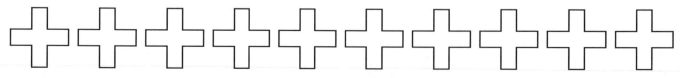

ODD AND EVEN NUMBERS
GIVE ME FIVE MENU

Objectives Covered Through This Menu and These Activities

- Students will distinguish odd and even numbers.
- Students will share different ways of identifying odd and even numbers.

Materials Needed by Students for Completion

- Poster board or large white paper
- DVD or VHS recorder (for commercials)
- Large blank or lined index cards (for instruction cards)
- Coat hangers (for mobiles)
- String (for mobiles)
- Blank index cards (for mobiles and trading cards)

Special Notes on the Use of This Menu

- This menu gives students the opportunity to create a commercial. Although students enjoy producing their own videos, there are often difficulties obtaining the equipment and scheduling the use of the video recorder. This activity can be modified by allowing students to act out the commercial (like a play) or, if students have the technology, allowing them to produce a Webcam or Flash version of their commercial.

Time Frame

- 1 week—Students are given the menu as the unit is started, and the teacher discusses all of the product options on the menu. As the different options are discussed, students will color or circle the graphic for each option that represents the activity they are most interested in completing based on a goal of five points. In this menu, that would imply students complete either two products (a two-point and a three-point) or one five-point product. As students complete products, they will color corresponding graphics along the bottom of the menu so they can track their progress toward their five-point goal. As the lessons progress throughout the week, the teacher and students refer back to the menu options associated with the content being taught. The teacher may choose to dedicate a learning center to working on menu products or simply allow time to work after other work is finished.

- 1–2 days—The teacher chooses an activity or product from the menu to use with the entire class.

Suggested Forms

- All-purpose rubric
- Free-choice proposal form if appropriate for content and level of students

Name:_____

ODD AND EVEN NUMBERS

Directions: Choose activities from the menu below. The activities must total 5. Place a check mark or color the picture next to each box to show which activities you will complete. Color the flowers along the bottom as you complete your activities to reach 5! All activities must be completed by _____.

2

 ❏ Make a set of **trading cards** for 5 even numbers and 5 odd numbers.

 ❏ Create an odd and even **mobile** with pictures of objects that come in odd numbers and even numbers.

3

 ❏ Write an **instruction card** that helps a student tell if a number is odd or even.

 ❏ Create a **folded quiz book** about odd and even numbers. Quiz your classmates on how to tell if a number is odd or even.

5

 ❏ They say that nature is full of more odd numbers than even ones. Write a **children's book** that shows examples of this.

 ❏ Write and perform a **play** about an odd number that wishes it was even. Be sure to include why the number wants to be even.

 ❏ Do you prefer odd or even numbers? Create a **commercial** for the type of numbers you like better. Include examples of and reasons for your choice in your commercial.

❏ **Free choice**—Submit a proposal form to your teacher for a product of your choice.

100TH DAY OF SCHOOL
2-5-8 MENU

Objectives Covered Through This Menu and These Activities
- Students will practice counting to 100.
- Students will identify 100 objects found around them.

Materials Needed by Students for Completion
- Poster board or large white paper
- Microsoft PowerPoint or other slideshow software
- Project Cube Template
- Plastic bags for collections

Time Frame
- 1–2 weeks—Students are given the menu as the unit is started, and the teacher discusses all of the product options on the menu. As the different options are discussed, students color or circle the graphic for each option that represents the activity they are most interested in completing so they meet their goal of 10 points. As students complete products, they will color corresponding graphics along the bottom of the menu so they can track their progress toward their 10-point goal. As the lessons progress through the week(s), the teacher and students refer back to the menu options associated with the content being taught.
- 1–2 days—The teacher chooses an activity or product from the menu to use with the entire class.

Suggested Forms
- All-purpose rubric
- Free-choice proposal form if appropriate for content and level of students

Name:_____

100TH DAY OF SCHOOL

Directions: Choose activities from the menu below. The activities must total 10 points. Place a check mark or color the picture next to each box to show which activities you will complete. Color the calendars along the bottom as you complete your activities to reach 10! All activities must be completed by

_____.

2 POINTS

❑ Start a **collection** of 100 things that can be put into a small plastic bag. Bring your collection to school.

❑ Look around your school or classroom and write a **list** of things that can be found in groups larger than 100.

5 POINTS

❑ Why is the 100th day of school special? Create an **advertisement** for 100th day. (Be sure to include 100 items on your ad!)

❑ Create a 100th-day **cube** with different activities that you could do to celebrate this day. Use the prompts on the cube to write your ideas.

❑ Create a **greeting card** to celebrate the 100th day of school. Include 100 items or decorations on the card.

❑ Because the 100th day celebrates the number 100, develop a **PowerPoint presentation** that shows how to count to 100 by 2's, 5's, and 10's.

8 POINTS

❑ Make a special plan for your 100th day where you will do exactly 100 things. Write a **diary** about the 100 things you did.

❑ **Free choice**—Submit a proposal form to your teacher for a product of your choice.

100TH-DAY CUBE

Create a 100th-day **cube** with different activities that you could do to celebrate. Use the prompts on the cube to write your ideas. Use this pattern or create your own cube.

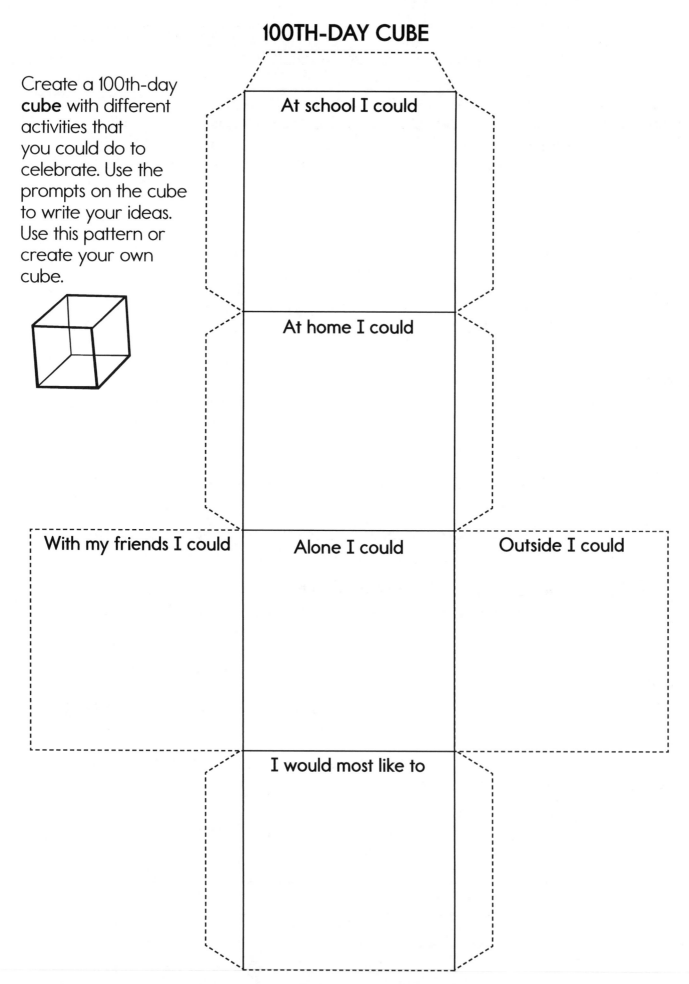

At school I could

At home I could

With my friends I could

Alone I could

Outside I could

I would most like to

GREATER THAN, LESS THAN GIVE ME FIVE MENU

Objectives Covered Through This Menu and These Activities

- Students will write number sentences showing the greater than and less than relationships.

Materials Needed by Students for Completion

- Poster board or large white paper
- Microsoft PowerPoint or other slideshow software
- Materials for class game (folders, colored cards, etc.)

Special Notes on the Use of This Menu

- This menu gives students the opportunity to demonstrate a concept. This can take a significant amount of time and organization. It can save time if the demonstration is recorded to share at a later time or if all of the students who choose to do a demonstration sign up for a designated day and time.

Time Frame

- 1 week—Students are given the menu as the unit is started, and the teacher discusses all of the product options on the menu. As the different options are discussed, students will color or circle the graphic for each option that represents the activity they are most interested in completing based on a goal of five points. In this menu, that would imply students complete either two products (a two-point and a three-point) or one five-point product. As students complete products, they will color corresponding graphics along the bottom of the menu so they can track their progress toward their five-point goal. As the lessons progress throughout the week, the teacher and students refer back to the menu options associated with the content being taught. The teacher may choose to dedicate a learning center to working on menu products or simply allow time to work after other work is finished.
- 1–2 days—The teacher chooses an activity or product from the menu to use with the entire class.

Suggested Forms

- All-purpose rubric
- Free-choice proposal form if appropriate for content and level of students

GREATER THAN, LESS THAN

Directions: Choose activities from the menu below. The activities must total 5. Place a check mark or color the picture next to each box to show which activities you will complete. Color the symbols along the bottom as you complete your activities to reach 5! All activities must be completed by _____.

2

❑ Create a **drawing** that shows how to choose whether to use the greater than or the less than symbol.

❑ Write three sentences that use the terms greater than or less than. Make each word sentence into a number sentence.

3

❑ Do a **demonstration** that shows how to use the greater than and less than symbols correctly in a number sentence with more than two numbers.

❑ **Free choice**—Submit a proposal form to your teacher for a product of your choice.

5

❑ Make a **class game** in which players guess if the number of something is greater than or less than 10. Include an answer key for your game.

❑ People say that for every greater than sentence, there is a less than sentence. Do you agree? Create a **PowerPoint presentation** that shows whether this is true or false.

BASIC FRACTIONS
THREE-SHAPE MENU

Objectives Covered Through This Menu and These Activities

- Students will state how fractions are used on a daily basis.
- Students will understand and represent commonly used fractions, such as ¼, ⅓, and ½.

Materials Needed by Students for Completion

- Poster board or large white paper
- Coat hangers (for mobiles)
- String (for mobiles)
- Blank index cards (for mobiles)
- Materials for bulletin board displays

Special Notes on the Use of This Menu

- This menu gives students the opportunity to demonstrate a concept. This can take a significant amount of time and organization. It can save time if the demonstration is recorded to share at a later time or if all of the students who choose to do a demonstration sign up for a designated day and time.
- This menu allows students to create a bulletin board display. Some classrooms may have only one bulletin board, so the teacher can divide the board into sections, or additional classroom wall or hall space can be sectioned off for the creation of these displays. Students can plan their displays based on the amount of space they are assigned.

Time Frame

- 1–3 weeks—Students are given the menu as the unit is started. As the unit progresses throughout the week, students should refer back to the menu options associated with that content. The teacher will go over all of the options for that content and have students circle the boxes that represent the activities they are most interested in completing. As teaching continues over the next 2–3 weeks, shapes will be colored in as each activity is completed. The activities should be completed in such a way that students complete one from each shape group. When students complete this pattern, they will have completed

one activity from each content area, learning style, or level of Bloom's Revised taxonomy, depending on the design of the menu.

- 1–2 days—The teacher chooses an activity or product from an objective to use with the entire class during that lesson time.

Suggested Forms

- All-purpose rubric
- Free-choice proposal form if appropriate for content and level of students

Name:_____

BASIC FRACTIONS

Directions: Complete three activities, one from each shape group. Circle the shapes you might like to do. Color in the shapes as you complete them. All activities must be completed by _____.

Make a **windowpane** with six pictures cut from magazines. Draw lines on the pictures to show examples of ½, ⅓, and ¼.

Create a **picture dictionary** for five common fractions.

Compose a fraction **song** about what fractions are with examples!

Create a **mobile** showing at least 10 different ways we use fractions in our daily lives.

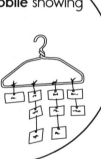

Write a **children's book** that teaches readers about fractions seen every day and how to divide objects into pieces.

Develop a **bulletin board display** with examples of fractions seen every day.

A friend always has trouble deciding whether to have ½ or ⅓ of a sandwich. Conduct a **demonstration** that shows how to decide between the two sizes of sandwich.

You are a superhero! Your superpowers allow you to turn whole numbers into fractions. Perform a **play** where your superpowers save the day!

Teachers always say "Fractions are our friends!" Make a **speech** to convince your classmates this is true.

PATTERNS
2–5–8 MENU

Objectives Covered Through This Menu and These Activities

- Students will sort, classify, and order objects by size, number, and other properties.
- Students will recognize, describe, and extend patterns such as sequences of sounds and shapes or simple numeric patterns and translate from one representation to another.
- Students will analyze how both repeating and growing patterns are generated.

Materials Needed by Students for Completion

- Poster board or large white paper
- Materials for board games (folders, colored cards, etc.)
- Materials for bulletin board displays
- Blank index cards (for concentration and trading cards)

Special Notes on the Use of This Menu

- This menu allows students to create a bulletin board display. Some classrooms may have only one bulletin board, so the teacher can divide the board into sections, or additional classroom wall or hall space can be sectioned off for the creation of these displays. Students can plan their displays based on the amount of space they are assigned.

Time Frame

- 1–2 weeks—Students are given the menu as the unit is started, and the teacher discusses all of the product options on the menu. As the different options are discussed, students color or circle the graphic for each option that represents the activity they are most interested in completing so they meet their goal of 10 points. As students complete products, they will color corresponding graphics along the bottom of the menu so they can track their progress toward their 10-point goal. As the lessons progress through the week(s), the teacher and students refer back to the menu options associated with the content being taught.
- 1–2 days—The teacher chooses an activity or product from the menu to use with the entire class.

Suggested Forms

- All-purpose rubric
- Free-choice proposal form if appropriate for content and level of students

Name:_____

PATTERNS

Directions: Choose activities from the menu below. The activities must total 10 points. Place a check mark or color the picture next to each box to show which activities you will complete. Color the checkerboard along the bottom as you complete your activities to reach 10! All activities must be completed by

_____.

2 POINTS

❏ Make a **collection** of at least 20 different items. Create a poster showing at least three different ways you could sort your collection and how your collection would look if it was sorted each way.

❏ Develop a set of **trading cards** about your favorite animals. Then come up with two different ways you could sort the cards. Write a sentence explaining why you chose to sort them that way.

5 POINTS

❏ Create a set of **concentration cards.** Each pair should have a number pattern on one of the cards and the next number in the series on the other card. Include an answer key!

❏ Develop a **bulletin board display** that shows different ways of sorting classroom objects.

❏ Create a **board game** that has players try to figure out hard number patterns. Be sure you have an answer key so they can check their answers!

❏ **Free choice**—Submit a proposal form to your teacher for a product of your choice.

8 POINTS

❏ Write a **children's book** about patterns we see in nature. Include lots of pictures as examples!

❏ Your teacher has decided that there will be homework every other day, starting today. Construct a plan that shows how many days you will have homework this week. Can you predict how many days you will have homework this month? This year? Show your predictions on a poster.

MONEY MEAL MENU

Objectives Covered Through This Menu and These Activities

- Students will describe the different coins and bills in the United States currency system.
- Students will express various uses for money, from spending to saving.

Materials Needed by Students for Completion

- Poster board or large white paper
- Scrapbooking materials
- Materials for money games (folders, colored cards, etc.)
- Project Cube Template
- Socks (for puppets)
- Paper bags (for puppets)
- Recycled materials (for puppets)
- Coat hangers (for mobiles)
- String (for mobiles)
- Blank index cards (for concentration cards and mobiles)

Special Notes on the Use of This Menu

- This menu asks students to use recycled materials. This does not mean only plastic and paper; instead, students should focus on using materials in new ways. It works well if a box is started for "recycled" contributions at the beginning of the school year. That way, students always have access to these types of materials.

Time Frame

- 1–3 weeks—Students are given the menu as the unit is started. As the unit progresses throughout the week, students should refer back to the menu options associated with that content. The teacher will go over all of the options for that content and have students color or circle the graphic for each option that represents the activity they are most interested in completing. As teaching continues over the next 2–3 weeks, the activities chosen and completed should create a full day's meal, with a breakfast, a lunch, a dinner, and an optional dessert. The teacher may choose to dedicate a learning center to working on menu products or simply allow time to work after other work is finished. When students complete the menu with this expectation, they have completed one activity from each content area, learning style, or level of Bloom's Revised taxonomy, depending on the design of the menu.

- 1–2 days—The teacher chooses an activity or product from an objective to use with the entire class during that lesson time.

Suggested Forms

- All-purpose rubric
- Free-choice proposal form if appropriate for content and level of students

MONEY

Directions: Choose one activity each for breakfast, lunch, and dinner. Dessert is an activity you can choose to do after you have finished your other meals. All activities must be completed by _____.

Breakfast

- Construct a money **mobile** that shows our money and its values.

- Create a set of **concentration cards** for money and its value.

- Read a library book about money. Design a **book cover** for the book you chose.

Lunch

- Read the fable of the ant and the grasshopper. Create a **puppet** for one of the characters out of recycled materials and retell the fable using money instead of food.

- Think about things that people *need* to buy rather than just *want* to buy. Design a **money cube** showing six different items that people need most.

- Create a **song or rap** about the importance of saving money.

Name: _____

Dinner

- Create a **children's book** that teaches about our money, its value, and how people use it.

- Design your own money **game** in which players learn about money and make choices about buying items.

- Make a **scrapbook** of items you could buy with $0.50, $1, $10, and $100.

Dessert

- Research a money system used in another country. Design a **poster** showing that country's system and comparing it to ours.

- Develop your own money. What would it look like and what would its value be? Make a **brochure** about your new money.

MONEY CUBE

There are lots of things that people buy. Some are things they need, and others are things they want. Think about things that people need. Make a **cube** and draw a picture of the six most important things people buy based on their needs. Use this pattern or create your own cube.

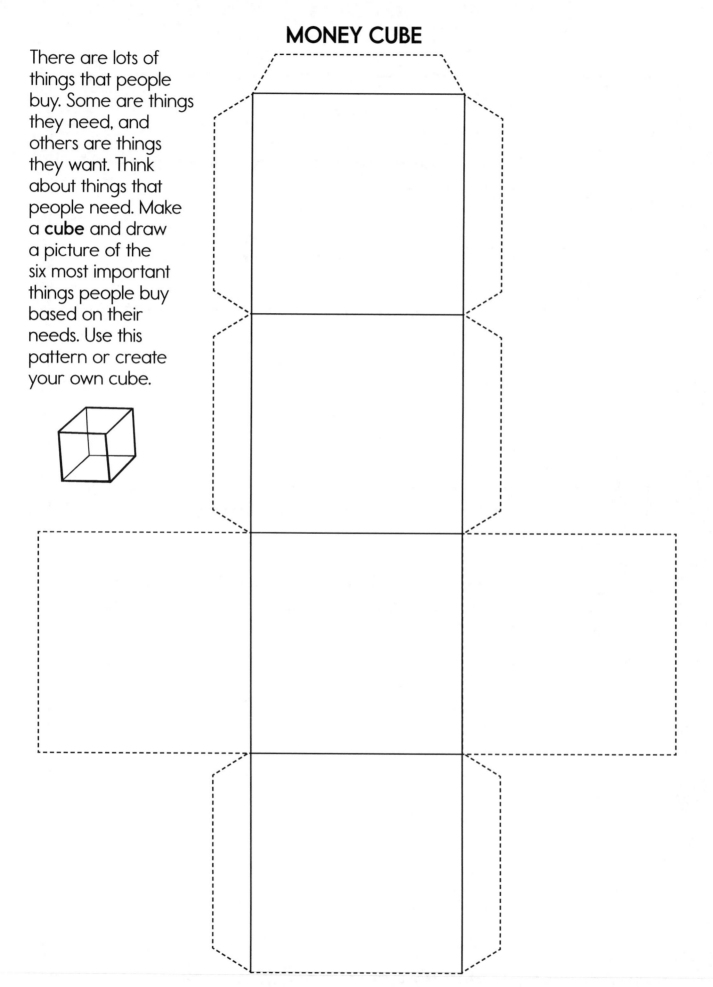

CHAPTER 6

Operations Menus

ADDITION
THREE-SHAPE MENU

Objectives Covered Through This Menu and These Activities
- Students will develop and use strategies for whole-number addition.
- Students will use a variety of computation methods and tools, including objects, paper and pencils, and calculators.

Materials Needed by Students for Completion
- Poster board or large white paper
- Materials for board games (folders, colored cards, etc.)
- Blank index cards (for concentration cards)

Time Frame
- 1–3 weeks—Students are given the menu as the unit is started. As the unit progresses throughout the week, students should refer back to the menu options associated with that content. The teacher will go over all of the options for that content and have students circle the boxes that represent the activities they are most interested in completing. As teaching continues over the next 2–3 weeks, shapes will be colored in as each activity is completed. The activities should be completed in such a way that students complete one from each shape group. When students complete this pattern, they will have completed one activity from each content area, learning style, or level of Bloom's Revised taxonomy, depending on the design of the menu.
- 1–2 days—The teacher chooses an activity or product from an objective to use with the entire class during that lesson time.

Suggested Forms
- All-purpose rubric
- Free-choice proposal form if appropriate for content and level of students

Name:_____

ADDITION

Directions: Choose one activity from each shape group. Circle one choice from each group of shapes. Color in the shape after you have finished it. All activities must be completed by _____.

Develop a **folded quiz book** with 10 different addition word problems on it. Include an answer key!

Make a set of **concentration cards** with an addition problem on one card and the answer on the other.

Create a **board game** in which players have to answer addition problems as they progress through the game.

Some people do not like word problems. Construct a **brochure** with suggestions to make addition word problems easier.

Perform a **song** about adding that includes at least two different word problems and how to solve them.

Create a **class game** to help your classmates practice answering addition word problems.

Write a **story** about a child who is having trouble adding numbers and how his or her friends help the child finally understand how to do it.

Perform a **play** about a person who is able to add in his or her head and why this is both a good and a bad thing.

Develop an **advertisement** for a machine that will answer addition problems. It is not like a calculator, because it will only do addition. Include how the machine works in your advertisement.

This page is intentionally left blank.

SUBTRACTION
POINT-BASED LIST MENU

Objectives Covered Through This Menu and These Activities

- Students will understand the effects of subtracting whole numbers.
- Students will complete basic subtraction problems including regrouping when appropriate.

Materials Needed by Students for Completion

- Poster board or large white paper
- Socks (for puppets)
- Paper bags (for puppets)
- Recycled materials (for puppets and models)
- Materials for bulletin board displays
- Materials for board games (folders, colored cards, etc.)

Special Notes on the Use of This Menu

- This menu asks students to use recycled materials. This does not mean only plastic and paper; instead, students should focus on using materials in new ways. It works well if a box is started for "recycled" contributions at the beginning of the school year. That way, students always have access to these types of materials.
- This menu allows students to create a bulletin board display. Some classrooms may have only one bulletin board, so the teacher can divide the board into sections, or additional classroom wall or hall space can be sectioned off for the creation of these displays. Students can plan their displays based on the amount of space they are assigned.

Time Frame

- 1–2 weeks—Students are given the menu as the unit is started, and the guidelines and target number of products are discussed. This menu has a point goal of 20, so 20/20 would represent 100%. There is also an opportunity for extra credit if the teacher would like to allow extra points. Because this menu covers one topic in depth, the teacher will go over all of the options on the menu and have students color the graphics or place check marks in the boxes next to the activities they are most interested in completing. Teachers will need to set aside a few moments to sign the agreement at the bottom of the page with each student. As instruction continues, activities are completed by students and submitted for grading. The teacher may choose to dedicate a learning center to working on menu products or simply allow time to work after other work is finished.

- 1–2 days—The teacher chooses an activity or product from an objective to use with the entire class during that lesson time.

Suggested Forms

- All-purpose rubric
- Free-choice proposal form if appropriate for content and level of students

Name:_____

SUBTRACTION

Guidelines:
1. You may complete as many of the activities listed as you can within the time period.
2. You may choose any combination of activities.
3. Your goal is 20 points.
4. You must show your plan to your teacher by _____.
5. Activities may be turned in at any time during the working time period. They will be graded and recorded on this sheet as you continue to work, so keep it safe!

Plan to Do	Activity to Complete	Point Value	Date Completed	Points Earned
	Create a **model** out of recycled materials that shows how subtraction works.	5		
	Design a **folded quiz book** with at least five different subtraction word problems to quiz your classmates. Don't forget the answer key!	5		
	Construct a set of **concentration cards** in which players match subtraction problems with the answers.	5		
	Create a **song** about 23 minus 5.	10		
	Write a **letter** to a family member telling whether or not you like subtraction. Include examples of problems in your letter so your family member knows how you feel.	10		
	Write a **children's book** about subtraction and how to solve subtraction problems.	10		
	Create a **bulletin board display** that another teacher could use with his or her students to teach the basics of subtraction.	10		
	Make an **advertisement** in which customers will save $8 on every purchase. Give examples of what they might buy.	10		
	The number 12 has just had 4 subtracted from it. Design a **greeting card** for the number 12 based on how it must be feeling.	10		
	Construct a **puppet** out of recycled materials to use in a puppet show that shows that subtraction happens every day, and not always in math problems!	15		
	Develop a subtraction **board game** in which everyone starts with the number 100 and the first person to reach zero wins!	15		
	Free choice—Submit a proposal form to your teacher for a product of your choice.	5–15		
	Total number of points you are planning to earn:		Total points earned:	

I am planning to complete ____ activities that could earn up to a total of ____ points.

Teacher's initials _____ Student's signature _____

BASIC ADDITION AND SUBTRACTION THREE-SHAPE MENU

Objectives Covered Through This Menu and These Activities

- Students will show the processes of addition and subtraction both in words and with pictures.
- Students will understand how addition and subtraction are related.
- Students will use addition and subtraction to solve word problems.
- Students will identify various fact families.

Materials Needed by Students for Completion

- Poster board or large white paper
- Large blank or lined index cards (for instruction cards)
- Microsoft PowerPoint or other slideshow software
- Project Cube Template
- Materials for board games (folders, colored cards, etc.)
- Magazines
- Blank index cards (for concentration cards)

Special Notes on the Use of This Menu

- This menu gives students the opportunity to demonstrate a concept. This can take a significant amount of time and organization. It can save time if the demonstration is recorded to share at a later time or if all of the students who choose to do a demonstration sign up for a designated day and time.

Time Frame

- 1–3 weeks—Students are given the menu as the unit is started. As the unit progresses throughout the week, students should refer back to the menu options associated with that content. The teacher will go over all of the options for that content and have students circle the boxes that represent the activities they are most interested in completing. As teaching continues over the next 2–3 weeks, shapes will be colored in as each activity is completed. The activities should be completed in such a way that students complete one from each shape group. When students complete this pattern, they will have completed

one activity from each content area, learning style, or level of Bloom's Revised taxonomy, depending on the design of the menu.

- 1–2 days—The teacher chooses an activity or product from an objective to use with the entire class during that lesson time.

Suggested Forms

- All-purpose rubric
- Free-choice proposal form if appropriate for content and level of students

Name:_____

BASIC ADDITION AND SUBTRACTION

Directions: Choose one activity from each shape group. Circle one choice from each group of shapes. Color in the shape after you have finished it. All activities must be completed by _____.

Write an **instruction card** that shows the processes of addition and subtraction using pictures and words.

Use **PowerPoint** (or another computer program) to show the processes of addition and subtraction using graphics and words.

Design a **children's book** that teaches the processes of addition and subtraction.

Make a problem **cube** with a different word problem on each side. Three of the problems should use addition to solve, and three should use subtraction.

Create a **board game** where players use addition and subtraction word problems to move forward. Be sure to include an answer key!

Using a magazine, find at least three pictures you like. Make up an addition and a subtraction word problem for each picture. Create a **mobile** of the pictures and the word problems.

Do a **demonstration** that shows how addition and subtraction are related. Be sure to include at least two examples!

Develop a set of **concentration cards** for three different fact families, using both addition and subtraction!

Make a **Venn diagram** to compare addition and subtraction.

WORD PROBLEM CUBE

Make a problem cube with a different word problem on each side. Three of the problems should use addition to solve, and three should use subtraction. Use this pattern or create your own cube.

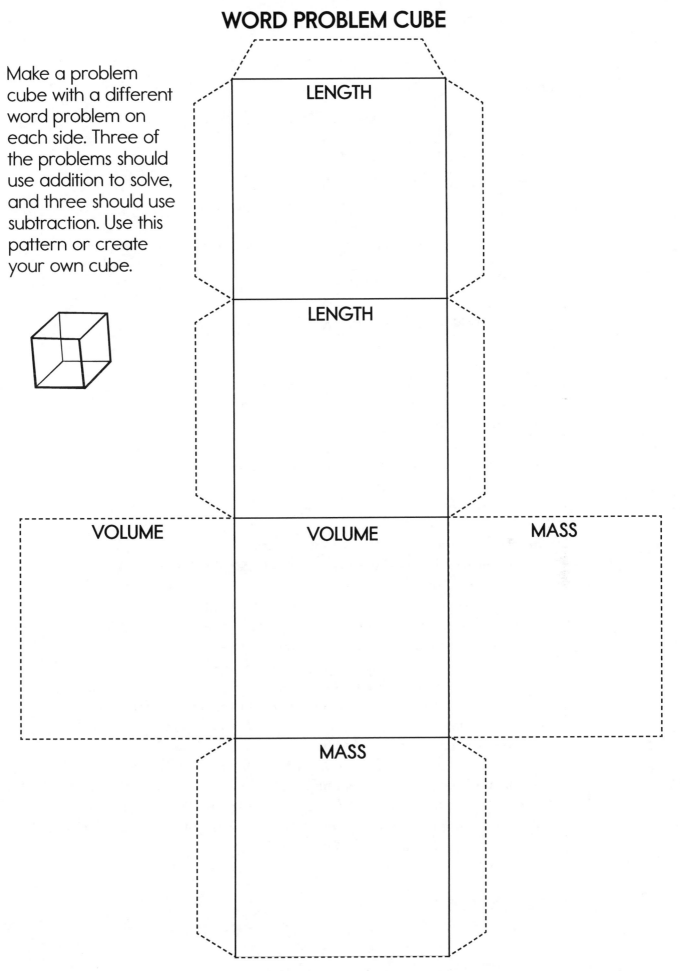

LENGTH

LENGTH

VOLUME **VOLUME** **MASS**

MASS

THE GROCERY STORE MEAL MENU

Objectives Covered Through This Menu and These Activities

- Students will understand that money is used to purchase grocery items.
- Students will investigate how to get the most for their money.
- Students will use mathematical functions to solve money-related problems.

Materials Needed by Students for Completion

- Advertisements from a grocery store
- Library books about children and money
- Recycled materials (for models and puppets)
- Socks (for puppets)
- Paper bags (for puppets)
- Poster board or large white paper
- Materials for board games (folders, colored cards, etc.)
- Magazines (for collages)
- Materials for bulletin board displays

Special Notes on the Use of This Menu

- This menu asks students to use recycled materials. This does not mean only plastic and paper; instead, students should focus on using materials in new ways. It works well if a box is started for "recycled" contributions at the beginning of the school year. That way, students always have access to these types of materials.
- This menu gives students the opportunity to demonstrate a concept. This can take a significant amount of time and organization. It can save time if the demonstration is recorded to share at a later time or if all of the students who choose to do a demonstration sign up for a designated day and time.
- This menu allows students to create a bulletin board display. Some classrooms may have only one bulletin board, so the teacher can divide the board into sections, or additional classroom wall or hall space can be sectioned off for the creation of these displays. Students can plan their display based on the amount of space they are assigned.

Time Frame

- 1–3 weeks—Students are given the menu as the unit is started. As the unit progresses throughout the week, students should refer back to the menu options associated with that content. The teacher will go over all of the options for that content and have students color or circle the graphic for each option that represents the activity they are most interested in completing. As teaching continues over the next 2–3 weeks, the activities chosen and completed should create a full day's meal, with a breakfast, a lunch, a dinner, and an optional dessert. The teacher may choose to dedicate a learning center to working on menu products or simply allow time to work after other work is finished. When students complete the menu with this expectation, they have completed one activity from each content area, learning style, or level of Bloom's Revised taxonomy, depending on the design of the menu.
- 1–2 days—The teacher chooses an activity or product from an objective to use with the entire class during that lesson time.

Suggested Forms

- All-purpose rubric
- Free-choice proposal form if appropriate for content and level of students

The Grocery Store

Directions: Choose one activity each for breakfast, lunch, and dinner. Dessert is an activity you can choose to do after you have finished your other meals. All activities must be completed by _____.

Breakfast

- Create a **collage** of the different types of things you can buy at a grocery store.

- Make a **mind map** for the major areas of a grocery store and what is found in each area.

- Design an **advertisement** for your local grocery store; include why someone might choose to shop there rather than at another store.

Lunch

- Using an advertisement from your local grocery store, create a **poster** of how you would spend $10. You need to buy at least 10 items.

- Design a **bulletin board display** using an advertisement from your local grocery store. Your bulletin board should ask math questions about items in the advertisement.

- Develop a **board game** in which players answer math questions using an advertisement from your grocery store.

Name:

Dinner

- Create a **puppet** out of recycled materials who wants to tell others about how to be a good shopper at the grocery store. Include examples!

- Design a **children's book** that shows how to save money at the grocery store.

- Using products from the grocery store, create a **demonstration** to show good shopping skills and ways to spend less but get more.

Dessert

- Read a library book about children and money. Design a **brochure** about the tips presented in the book.

- Using recycled materials, make a **model** of your perfect grocery store. What types of products would it carry, and how would it be arranged?

CHAPTER 7

 Geometry Menus

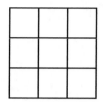

BASIC SHAPES
TIC-TAC-TOE MENU

Objectives Covered Through This Menu and These Activities

- Students will identify basic shapes.
- Students will use basic shapes in creative ways.

Materials Needed by Students for Completion

- Poster board or large white paper
- Materials for board games (folders, colored cards, etc.)
- Coat hangers (for mobiles)
- String (for mobiles)
- Blank index cards (for mobiles)
- Magazines (for collages)
- Count the Shapes worksheet

Special Notes on the Use of This Menu

- The answers for the Count the Shapes worksheet are: circles: 9; squares: 10; triangles: 10; and stars: 4.

Time Frame

- 2–3 weeks—Students are given the menu as the unit is started. As the teacher presents lessons throughout the week, he or she should refer back to the menu options associated with that content. The teacher will go over all of the options for that content and have students place check marks in the boxes that represent the activities they are most interested in completing. As teaching continues over the next 2–3 weeks, activities chosen and completed should make a column or row. The teacher may choose to dedicate a learning center to working on menu products or simply allow time to work after other work is finished. When students complete this pattern, they will have completed one activity from each content area, learning style, or level of Bloom's Revised taxonomy, depending on the design of the menu.
- 1 week—At the start of the unit, the teacher chooses the three activities he or she feels are most valuable for students. Stations can be set up in the classroom. These three activities are available for student choice throughout the week as regular instruction takes place.

- 1–2 days—The teacher chooses an activity from the menu to use with the entire class.

Suggested Forms

- All-purpose rubric
- Free-choice proposal form if appropriate for content and level of students

Name:_____

BASIC SHAPES

Directions: Check the boxes you plan to complete. They should form a tic-tac-toe across or down. All activities must be completed by _____.

List and draw the shapes you will use in this menu here:

☐ **What Is That Shape?**	☐ **Having Fun With Shapes**	☐ **Using Shapes**
Construct a **windowpane** with a basic shape in each box.	Design an **advertisement** for your favorite shape. Tell why it is the best!	Create a **drawing** using at least 5 circles, 3 squares, 2 triangles, and 4 stars. Use only those shapes to make your drawing.
☐ **Using Shapes**	☐ **What Is That Shape?**	☐ **Having Fun With Shapes**
Design a shape **board game** that has players guess shapes.	Make a **mobile** of the basic shapes with examples we might see every day.	Create a **song** with hand motions to teach the basic shapes.
☐ **Having Fun With Shapes**	☐ **Using Shapes**	☐ **What Is That Shape?**
Complete the Count the Shapes activity.	Create a **children's book** that teaches the basic shapes.	Using pictures from magazines, design a **collage** of basic shapes seen in photos. Label each shape.

Name:_____

COUNT THE SHAPES

Directions: Record the number of each shape found in the items below. You may want to color or draw them as you count!

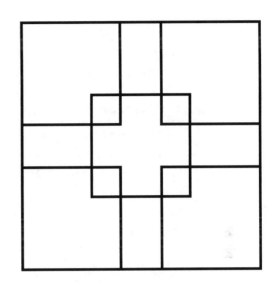

How many circles are there? _____   How many squares are there? _____

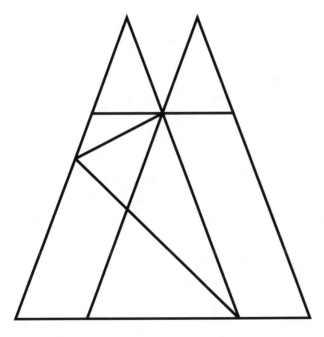

How many triangles are there? _____   How many stars are there? _____

SPACE FIGURES THREE-SHAPE MENU

Objectives Covered Through This Menu and These Activities

- Students will identify and compare various space figures including rectangular prisms, cubes, cylinders, cones, and spheres.

Materials Needed by Students for Completion

- Pattern blocks
- Socks (for puppets)
- Paper bags (for puppets)
- Recycled materials (for puppets)
- Ruler (for comic strip)
- Magazines (for collage)

Special Notes on the Use of This Menu

- This menu asks students to use recycled materials. This does not mean only plastic and paper; instead, students should focus on using materials in new ways. It works well if a box is started for "recycled" contributions at the beginning of the school year. That way, students always have access to these types of materials.

Time Frame

- 1–3 weeks—Students are given the menu as the unit is started. As the unit progresses throughout the week, students should refer back to the menu options associated with that content. The teacher will go over all of the options for that content and have students circle the boxes that represent the activities they are most interested in completing. As teaching continues over the next 2–3 weeks, shapes will be colored in as each activity is completed. The activities should be completed in such a way that students complete one from each shape group. When students complete this pattern, they will have completed one activity from each content area, learning style, or level of Bloom's Revised taxonomy, depending on the design of the menu.
- 1–2 days—The teacher chooses an activity or product from an objective to use with the entire class during that lesson time.

Suggested Forms

- All-purpose rubric
- Free-choice proposal form if appropriate for content and level of students

SPACE FIGURES

Directions: Choose one activity from each shape group. Circle one choice from each group of shapes. Color in the shape after you have finished it. All activities must be completed by _____.

Write all of the space figures you need to include in this menu:

Choose one of the space figures. Create a **comic strip** that shows examples of how the figure is used in our daily lives.

Write a **song or rap** using all of the space figures listed above.

Make a **collage** with pictures of objects with the space figure shapes. Label the pictures.

Construct a **folded quiz book** with riddles for each of the 3-D shapes.

Pretend you are one of the space figures listed above. Make a **Venn diagram** to compare and contrast yourself to another space figure.

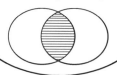

Create a **product cube** with clues to six different space figures. Make your clues tricky so your classmates really have to think about them!

Use pattern or shape blocks to make a new creature. Make a **drawing** of your creature and list all of the space figures you used to create it.

Design a space figure **puppet** using recycled materials. Have it tell your classmates about itself and explain why it is the best space figure of all.

Keep a space figure **diary** where you record every space figure you see for an entire day. Record the object, what figure it was, and where you saw it. See how many you can find!

SPACE FIGURES CUBE

List and number
your space figures.
Write clues on each
side of the **cube**
so your classmates
can guess what
that space figure
might be. Make
your clues tricky
so your classmates
really have to think
about them! Use this
pattern or create
your own cube.

Answer Key:

Space Figure 1:

Space Figure 2:

Space Figure 3:

Space Figure 4:

Space Figure 5:

Space Figure 6:

Space Figure 1

Space Figure 2

Space Figure 3

Space Figure 4

Space Figure 5

Space Figure 6

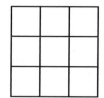

MAKING GRAPHS
TIC-TAC-TOE MENU

Objectives Covered Through This Menu and These Activities

- Students will create bar, picture, and circle graphs based on data.

Materials Needed by Students for Completion

- Poster board or large white paper
- Magazines (for collages)
- Recycled materials (for dioramas)

Special Notes on the Use of This Menu

- This menu gives students the opportunity to demonstrate a concept. This can take a significant amount of time and organization. It can save time if the demonstration is recorded to share at a later time or if all of the students who choose to do a demonstration sign up for a designated day and time.
- This menu asks students to use recycled materials. This does not mean only plastic and paper; instead, students should focus on using materials in new ways. It works well if a box is started for "recycled" contributions at the beginning of the school year. That way, students always have access to these types of materials.

Time Frame

- 2–3 weeks—Students are given the menu as the unit is started. As the teacher presents lessons throughout the week, he or she should refer back to the menu options associated with that content. The teacher will go over all of the options for that content and have students place check marks in the boxes that represent the activities they are most interested in completing. As teaching continues over the next 2–3 weeks, activities chosen and completed should make a column or row. The teacher may choose to dedicate a learning center to working on menu products or simply allow time to work after other work is finished. When students complete this pattern, they will have completed one activity from each content area, learning style, or level of Bloom's Revised taxonomy, depending on the design of the menu.
- 1 week—At the start of the unit, the teacher chooses the three activities he or she feels are most valuable for students. Stations can be set

up in the classroom. These three activities are available for student choice throughout the week as regular instruction takes place.

- 1–2 days—The teacher chooses an activity from the menu to use with the entire class.

Suggested Forms

- All-purpose rubric
- Free-choice proposal form if appropriate for content and level of students

Name:_____

MAKING GRAPHS

Directions: Check the boxes you plan to complete. They should form a tic-tac-toe across or down. All activities must be completed by _____.

☐ **Making a Circle Graph** Choose your favorite storybook. On a **poster**, create a graph that shows the amount of time your characters spend doing each of the activities in the story. 	☐ **Making a Bar Graph** Develop a classroom **demonstration** to show how to make a bar graph. Choose classroom objects to use for the graph in your demonstration. 	☐ **Making a Picture Graph** Write your own **children's book** about a picture graph. First, design your graph, and then write the story to match the pictures in the graph. 
☐ **Making a Picture Graph** Talk to the other students in your class about what they like to do on the weekend. Using magazines, create a **collage** picture graph that shows what you discovered. 	☐ **Free Choice on Creating a Circle Graph** (Fill out your proposal form before beginning the free choice!) 	☐ **Making a Bar Graph** Create a **book cover** for your favorite book. Include a bar graph about the characters, their clothes, or their actions. 
☐ **Making a Bar Graph** Using recycled materials, create a **diorama** of the ocean or fresh water with the plants and animals found there. Draw a bar graph that shows the number of living things in your diorama. 	☐ **Making a Picture Graph** Choose a nonfiction book. After **list**ing information from the book, make a picture graph to show the types of people, animals, or locations shown in the book. 	☐ **Making a Circle Graph** Choose four of your favorite topics. While you are at the library, locate the number of books your library has on each topic. Make an **advertisement** for the library that has a circle graph to show your information.

READING GRAPHS
THREE-SHAPE MENU

Objectives Covered Through This Menu and These Activities
- Students will make predictions and draw conclusions based on graphs.
- Students will read bar, circle, and picture graphs.

Materials Needed by Students for Completion
- Game Graphs worksheet
- Match It Graphing Activity worksheet
- Poster board or large white paper
- Materials for bulletin board displays
- Graph paper
- Scrapbooking materials
- Materials for board games (folders, colored cards, etc.)

Special Notes on the Use of This Menu
- This menu allows students to create a bulletin board display. Some classrooms may have only one bulletin board, so the teacher can divide the board into sections, or additional classroom wall or hall space can be sectioned off for the creation of these displays. Students can plan their displays based on the amount of space they are assigned.

Time Frame
- 1–3 weeks—Students are given the menu as the unit is started. As the unit progresses throughout the week, students should refer back to the menu options associated with that content. The teacher will go over all of the options for that content and have students circle the boxes that represent the activities they are most interested in completing. As teaching continues over the next 2–3 weeks, shapes will be colored in as each activity is completed. The activities should be completed in such a way that students complete one from each shape group. When students complete this pattern, they will have completed one activity from each content area, learning style, or level of Bloom's Revised taxonomy, depending on the design of the menu.
- 1–2 days—The teacher chooses an activity or product from an objective to use with the entire class during that lesson time.

Suggested Forms

- All-purpose rubric
- Free-choice proposal form if appropriate for content and level of students

Name:_____

READING GRAPHS

Directions: Choose one activity from each shape group. Circle one choice from each group of shapes. Color in the shape after you have finished it. All activities must be completed by _____.

Create a **brochure** with examples of the different types of graphs and instructions telling how to read them.

Choose the kind of graph that you think is the most difficult to understand. Develop a **poster** that shows how to read it. Write a paragraph on the back of the poster that explains why you think it is the hardest graph to read.

Write a **children's book** about graphs and how to read them. Choose graphs about topics that interest others your age.

Find an example of each type of graph you are studying. Create a **bulletin board display** that shares the graphs and what each shows.

Using the Game Graphs worksheet, develop a **board game** in which players answer questions about the graphs.

Look through your textbooks or books from the library to find a graph. Using graph paper, remake the graph and write a **paragraph** to explain what the graph shows.

The sky is blue today. I see a boat on the lake and a man fishing. There is a bird singing in the tree outside my window. I will soon eat breakfast and go for a bike ride with my friend Julie.

Write a **story** to match the graph shown on the Match It Graphing Activity worksheet. Continue your story for 2 days after the graph ends.

Design a **scrapbook** of graphs you find in newspapers or magazines. Write two sentences about each graph and add two pieces of additional information, such as more bars, pictures, or lines.

Free choice—Submit a proposal form to your teacher for a product of your choice.

Name:_____

MATCH IT GRAPHING ACTIVITY

Directions: Look at the picture graph below. Use the graph to predict and fill in Thursday and Friday. Write a story to match the information presented in the graph, including your predictions for the rest of the week.

Time Spent on Homework Each Day

Monday	 ✏️ ✏️ ✏️ ✏️ ✏️
Tuesday	 ✏️ ✏️ ✏️ ✏️
Wednesday	 ✏️ ✏️ ✏️
Thursday	
Friday	

Each pencil stands for 5 minutes of time.

Name:_____

GAME GRAPHS

Directions: Develop questions about the following graphs for your game. Be as creative as you like with the questions!

Students and Their Pets

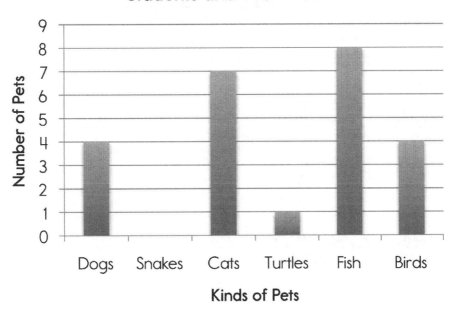

Favorite Subjects in School

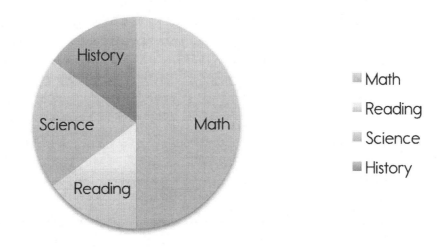

PERIMETER
GIVE ME FIVE MENU

Objectives Covered Through This Menu and These Activities

- Students will measure and calculate the perimeter of various regular and irregular objects.
- Students will understand that perimeter is the distance around an object.

Materials Needed by Students for Completion

- Poster board or large white paper
- Large blank or lined index cards (for instruction cards)
- Project Cube Template
- Recycled materials (for models)

Special Notes on the Use of This Menu

- This menu asks students to use recycled materials. This does not mean only plastic and paper; instead, students should focus on using materials in new ways. It works well if a box is started for "recycled" contributions at the beginning of the school year. That way, students always have access to these types of materials.

Time Frame

- 1 week—Students are given the menu as the unit is started, and the teacher discusses all of the product options on the menu. As the different options are discussed, students will color or circle the graphic for each option that represents the activity they are most interested in completing based on a goal of five points. In this menu, that would imply students complete either two products (a two-point and a three-point) or one five-point product. As students complete products, they will color corresponding graphics along the bottom of the menu so they can track their progress toward their five-point goal. As the lessons progress throughout the week, the teacher and students refer back to the menu options associated with the content being taught. The teacher may choose to dedicate a learning center to working on menu products or simply allow time to work after other work is finished.
- 1–2 days—The teacher chooses an activity or product from the menu to use with the entire class.

Suggested Forms

- All-purpose rubric
- Free-choice proposal form if appropriate for content and level of students

Name:_____

PERIMETER

Directions: Choose activities from the menu below. The activities must total 5. Place a check mark or color the picture next to each box to show which activities you will complete. Color the rulers along the bottom as you complete your activities to reach 5! All activities must be completed by

_____.

2

 ❏ Write an **instruction card** that tells how to measure the perimeter of different shapes.

❏ Create a **flipbook** of shapes whose perimeters we can easily measure. Draw the shape on the front, and write how to find the perimeter on the inside.

3

❏ Find three objects in the room with perimeters of about 50 cm, 72 cm, and 2 meters. Make a **list** of all the items you measured before you found three with these measurements.

❏ Construct a perimeter **cube** with six different word problems, one on each side.

 ❏ Choose an irregularly shaped figure in your classroom. Develop a plan for calculating the perimeter, and then find the perimeter. Show your results in a **drawing**.

5

 ❏ What is the perimeter (or circumference) of the Earth? Research how it is calculated. Create a **model** out of recycled materials that shows how we can calculate the perimeter of other large, spherical objects.

 ❏ Scale is used on maps to show large distances. Using a map of your state, calculate its perimeter. Design a **bulletin board** display that shows step-by-step how to do the calculations.

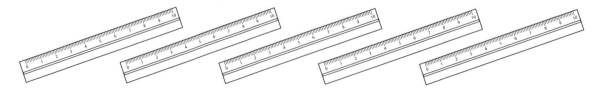

PERIMETER CUBE

Make a **cube** with six different word problem, one on each side. The number on the top has to be the answer to your problem, so think carefully! Use this pattern or create your own cube.

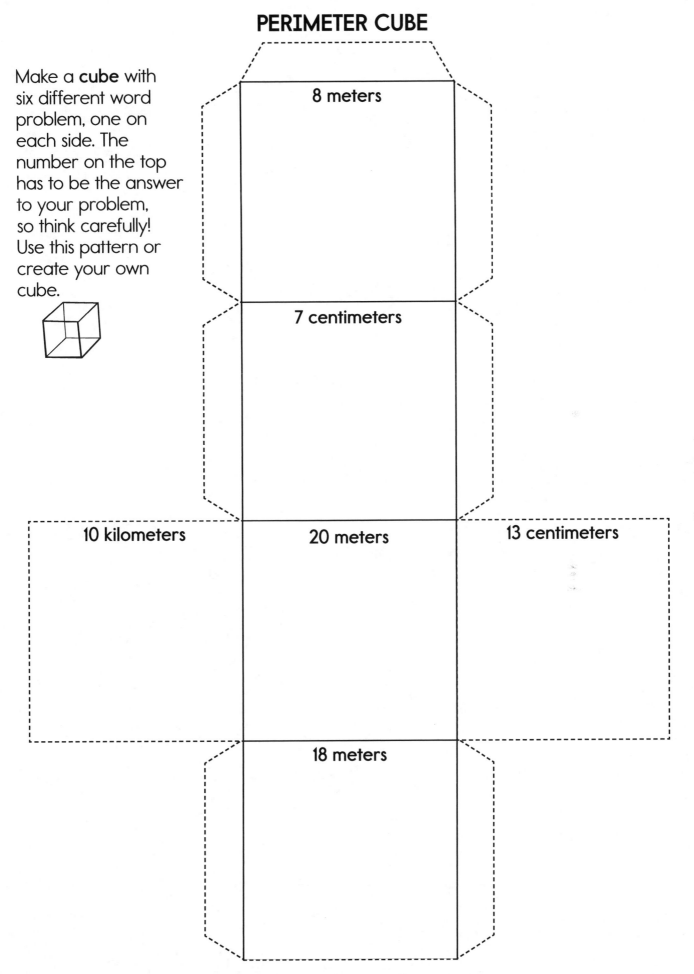

8 meters

7 centimeters

10 kilometers   20 meters   13 centimeters

18 meters

CHAPTER 8

Measurement Menus

CALENDAR MEAL MENU

Objectives Covered Through This Menu and These Activities

- Students will name the months of the year in order.
- Students will share activities done in each month.
- Students will investigate the origins of the names of our months and other historical calendars (optional).

Materials Needed by Students for Completion

- Poster board or large white paper
- Microsoft PowerPoint or other slideshow software
- Socks (for puppets)
- Paper bags (for puppets)
- Recycled materials (for puppets)

Special Notes on the Use of This Menu

- This menu gives students the opportunity to demonstrate a concept. This can take a significant amount of time and organization. It can save time if the demonstration is recorded to share at a later time or if all of the students who choose to do a demonstration sign up for a designated day and time.
- This menu asks students to use recycled materials. This does not mean only plastic and paper; instead, students should focus on using materials in new ways. It works well if a box is started for "recycled" contributions at the beginning of the school year. That way, students always have access to these types of materials.

Time Frame

- 1–3 weeks—Students are given the menu as the unit is started. As the unit progresses throughout the week, students should refer back to the menu options associated with that content. The teacher will go over all of the options for that content and have students color or circle the graphic for each option that represents the activity they are most interested in completing. As teaching continues over the next 2–3 weeks, the activities chosen and completed should create a full day's meal, with a breakfast, a lunch, a dinner, and an optional dessert. The teacher may choose to dedicate a learning center to working on menu products or simply allow time to work after other work is finished. When students complete the menu with this expectation, they have completed one activity from each content area, learning style, or level of Bloom's Revised taxonomy, depending on the design of the menu.

- 1–2 days—The teacher chooses an activity or product from an objective to use with the entire class during that lesson time.

Suggested Forms

- All-purpose rubric
- Free-choice proposal form if appropriate for content and level of students

CALENDAR

Directions: Choose one activity each for breakfast, lunch, and dinner. Dessert is an activity you can choose to do after you have finished your other meals. All activities must be completed by _____.

Breakfast

- Design a **windowpane** with 12 squares. Write one month in each square, and draw a picture for each one.

- Write an **alphabet book** about the months of the year.

- Create a **collage** with pictures for each month of the year. Label the pictures with the months.

Lunch

- Design your own calendar using pictures or **drawings**. Include all of the months.

- Write a **play** about the month that you like the best. Include what you like to do during that month and why it is your favorite.

- September has decided it is the best month of the year. However, October thinks it is the best. Using recycled materials, create a **puppet** for one of the months and share your ideas in a puppet show.

Name: _____

Dinner

- Here is a riddle for you to solve: How many months have 28 days? Find the correct answer and design a **poster** to prove your answer is correct.

- Would it be better to be paid every other week for a year, or on the 15th and 30th of every month for 12 months? Develop a **demonstration** to prove which is better.

- Keep a **diary** every day for a week. Be sure to record what day it is each day and what you did that was special!

Dessert

- Research the history of the names of our months. Make a **PowerPoint presentation** to share the information.

- Research different kinds of calendars from different civilizations in history and design a **book cover** for a book about the different calendars.

NONSTANDARD MEASUREMENT GIVE ME FIVE MENU

Objectives Covered Through This Menu and These Activities
- Students will understand how to measure using nonstandard and standard units.
- Students will measure with multiple copies of units of the same size.

Materials Needed by Students for Completion
- Poster board or large white paper
- Paperclips
- Rulers, meter sticks

Time Frame
- 1 week—Students are given the menu as the unit is started, and the teacher discusses all of the product options on the menu. As the different options are discussed, students will color or circle the graphic for each option that represents the activity they are most interested in completing based on a goal of five points. In this menu, that would imply students complete either two products (a two-point and a three-point) or one five-point product. As students complete products, they will color corresponding graphics along the bottom of the menu so they can track their progress toward their five-point goal. As the lessons progress throughout the week, the teacher and students refer back to the menu options associated with the content being taught. The teacher may choose to dedicate a learning center to working on menu products or simply allow time to work after other work is finished.
- 1–2 days—The teacher chooses an activity or product from the menu to use with the entire class.

Suggested Forms
- All-purpose rubric
- Free-choice proposal form if appropriate for content and level of students

Name:_____

NONSTANDARD MEASUREMENT

Directions: Choose activities from the menu below. The activities must total 5. Place a check mark or color the picture next to each box to show which activities you will complete. Color the hands along the bottom as you complete your activities to reach 5! All activities must be completed by

_____.

2

❏ Choose five large items in your classroom to measure using a paperclip. **List** each item and its measurements in paperclips.

❏ Gather a **collection** of items that are between two and four paperclips long.

3

❏ The height of a horse is measured in hands. Create a **brochure** that tells other nonstandard ways that objects are measured.

❏ Draw a **map** of your school showing the distances from your classroom to the gym, the library, and cafeteria. Use the number of steps to show distance on your map.

5

❏ Measure the length of your desk in paperclips and centimeters. Develop a plan to figure out how many paperclips it would take to go from your desk to the cafeteria. Design a **poster** that shows your plan.

❏ Create your own measurement system using an everyday object as its basic unit. Write a **children's book** about your system and how to use it to measure various objects.

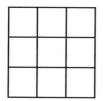

MEASUREMENT TIC-TAC-TOE MENU

Objectives Covered Through This Menu and These Activities

- Students will measure an object's length, width, and height.
- Students will express the weight of an object.
- Students will understand and express the volume of a container.

Materials Needed by Students for Completion

- Poster board or large white paper
- Materials for bulletin board displays
- Large blank or lined index cards (for instruction cards)
- Blank index cards (for trading cards)

Special Notes on the Use of This Menu

- This menu gives students the opportunity to demonstrate a concept. This can take a significant amount of time and organization. It can save time if the demonstration is recorded to share at a later time or if all of the students who choose to do a demonstration sign up for a designated day and time.
- This menu allows students to create a bulletin board display. Some classrooms may have only one bulletin board, so the teacher can divide the board into sections, or additional classroom wall or hall space can be sectioned off for the creation of these displays. Students can plan their displays based on the amount of space they are assigned.

Time Frame

- 2–3 weeks—Students are given the menu as the unit is started. As the teacher presents lessons throughout the week, he or she should refer back to the menu options associated with that content. The teacher will go over all of the options for that content and have students place check marks in the boxes that represent the activities they are most interested in completing. As teaching continues over the next 2–3 weeks, activities chosen and completed should make a column or row. The teacher may choose to dedicate a learning center to working on menu products or simply allow time to work after other work is finished. When students complete this pattern, they will have completed

one activity from each content area, learning style, or level of Bloom's Revised taxonomy, depending on the design of the menu.

- 1 week—At the start of the unit, the teacher chooses the three activities he or she feels are most valuable for students. Stations can be set up in the classroom. These three activities are available for student choice throughout the week as regular instruction takes place.
- 1–2 days—The teacher chooses an activity from the menu to use with the entire class.

Suggested Forms

- All-purpose rubric
- Free-choice proposal form if appropriate for content and level of students

Name:_____

MEASUREMENT

Directions: Check the boxes you plan to complete. They should form a tic-tac-toe across or down. All activities must be completed by _____.

☐ **Measuring Length**	☐ **Measuring Volume**	☐ **Measuring Weight**
Write an **instruction card** that explains how you could measure your height without any help from another person. Try your plan and record your height. 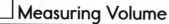	Design a set of **trading cards** for all of the different tools that can measure volume.	Create a **class game** in which your classmates make predictions and practice measuring the weight of classroom items. 
☐ **Measuring Weight**	☐ **Free Choice on Measuring Length**	☐ **Measuring Volume**
Write your own **children's book** about how to weigh objects and how much different objects weigh. Include both small and large objects in your book!	(Fill out your proposal form before beginning the free choice!) **Free**	Design a **bulletin board display** that shows at least four different ways to measure the volume of an object or liquid.
☐ **Measuring Volume**	☐ **Measuring Weight**	☐ **Measuring Length**
Create a **mind map** for measuring volume. 	Develop a **demonstration** to teach your classmates how to use different tools to weigh classroom items. 	Design a **windowpane** for six rectangular classroom items. Measure the length and width of each object and record the information in the windowpane.

TEMPERATURE
TARGET-BASED LIST MENU

Objectives Covered Through This Menu and These Activities

- Students will read temperature using a thermometer.
- Students will distinguish temperatures that seem hot and cold.
- Students will share how they measure and use temperatures in their daily lives.

Materials Needed by Students for Completion

- Poster board or large white paper
- Coat hangers (for mobiles)
- String (for mobiles)
- Blank index cards (for mobiles)
- Scrapbooking materials
- Socks (for puppets)
- Paper bags (for puppets)
- Recycled materials (for puppets)
- Thermometers
- Materials for board games (folders, colored cards, etc.)
- Blank index cards (for concentration cards)
- Large blank or lined index cards (for instruction cards)

Special Notes on the Use of This Menu

- This menu asks students to use recycled materials. This does not mean only plastic and paper; instead, students should focus on using materials in new ways. It works well if a box is started for "recycled" contributions at the beginning of the school year. That way, students always have access to these types of materials.

Time Frame

- 1–2 weeks—Students are given the menu as the unit is started and the guidelines and target number of products are discussed. This menu has an open blank on the top so teachers can designate their own target values based on time and knowledge of the students. A target number of four is a good place to begin, and teachers can adjust based on student expertise. There is also an opportunity for extra credit if the teacher would like to use another target number. Because this menu covers one topic in depth, the teacher will go over all of the options on the menu and have students color the graphics or place check marks in the boxes next to the activities they are most interested in completing. Teachers will need to set aside a few moments to sign the agreement at the bottom of the page with each student. As instruction continues, activities are completed by students and submitted for grading. The teacher may choose to dedicate a learning center to working on menu products or simply allow time to work after other work is finished.

- 1–2 days—The teacher chooses an activity or product from an objective to use with the entire class during that lesson time.

Suggested Forms

- All-purpose rubric
- Free-choice proposal form if appropriate for content and level of students

Name:_____

TEMPERATURE

Guidelines:
1. You may complete as many of the activities listed as you can within the time period.
2. You may choose any combination of activities. Your goal is to complete _____ activities.
3. You may be as creative as you like within the guidelines listed below.
4. You must share your plan with your teacher by _____.

Plan to Do	Activity to Complete	Completed
	Pretend you are a Fahrenheit thermometer; write an **instruction card** that explains how to find your temperature. What are considered hot and cold temperatures?	
	Keep a **diary** or journal of the daily temperatures for a week.	
	Design a set of **concentration cards** that matches temperatures with their readings on thermometers.	
	Create a **brochure** that explains how to use and read a thermometer.	
	Design a thermometer **puppet** out of recycled materials. Use your puppet in a puppet show to tell how temperature is important in our daily lives.	
	Create a **scrapbook** that has a temperature on the top of each page and pictures of what you like to do on days with that temperature.	
	Develop a **board game** in which players practice reading thermometers.	
	Perform a funny **play** about a child who confuses a Celsius thermometer with a Fahrenheit one and how it affects his or her plans for the day.	
	Come to class as a meteorologist and perform a **You Be the Person presentation** about the weather and the temperatures we can expect in the next week.	
	When people cook or bake, they use various temperatures. Make a **drawing** that shows the cooking temperatures of different foods. Be sure to include a food at the lowest temperature used for cooking or baking and a food for the highest temperature.	
	Design a **mobile** showing the different ways that people use temperature readings.	
	Write a **newspaper article** in which temperature plays the most important part of the story.	
	Free choice—Submit a proposal form to your teacher for a product of your choice.	
	Total number of activities you are planning to complete:	Total number of activities completed:

I am planning to complete _____ activities.

Teacher's initials _____ Student's signature _____

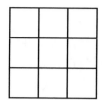

TIME
TIC-TAC-TOE MENU

Objectives Covered Through This Menu and These Activities

- Students will tell time using an analog clock.
- Students will track and predict elapsed time.

Materials Needed by Students for Completion

- Poster board or large white paper
- Blank index cards (for concentration cards)
- Materials for board games (folders, colored cards, etc.)
- Scrapbooking materials

Time Frame

- 2–3 weeks—Students are given the menu as the unit is started. As the teacher presents lessons throughout the week, he or she should refer back to the menu options associated with that content. The teacher will go over all of the options for that content and have students place check marks in the boxes that represent the activities they are most interested in completing. As teaching continues over the next 2–3 weeks, activities chosen and completed should make a column or row. The teacher may choose to dedicate a learning center to working on menu products or simply allow time to work after other work is finished. When students complete this pattern, they will have completed one activity from each content area, learning style, or level of Bloom's Revised taxonomy, depending on the design of the menu.
- 1 week—At the start of the unit, the teacher chooses the three activities he or she feels are most valuable for students. Stations can be set up in the classroom. These three activities are available for student choice throughout the week as regular instruction takes place.
- 1–2 days—The teacher chooses an activity from the menu to use with the entire class.

Suggested Forms

- All-purpose rubric
- Free-choice proposal form if appropriate for content and level of students

Name:_____

TIME

Directions: Check the boxes you plan to complete. They should form a tic-tac-toe across or down. All activities must be completed by _____.

☐ **Why Time Is Important** Write a **story** about a person who doesn't know how to tell time and how this affects his or her life. 	☐ **Telling Time** Create a **board game** using clock drawings so your classmates can practice telling time. 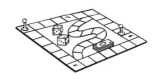	☐ **Passing Time** Make a **scrapbook** of activities that can be done in 5 minutes or less, 15–30 minutes, and an hour. 
☐ **Passing Time** Create a set of **concentration cards** where players match two items with the amount of time passing between them. 	☐ **Free Choice** (Fill out your proposal form before beginning the free choice!) Free	☐ **Telling Time** There are different ways to say the same time. Design a **windowpane** telling all of the ways you could express this time: 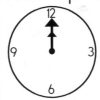
☐ **Telling Time** Write a **children's book** that teaches others how to read a clock. 	☐ **Passing Time** Develop a schedule for your perfect day that includes what you would do at certain times and how much time would be spent on each activity. Put your schedule on a **poster**. 	☐ **Why Time Is Important** Why should we learn to tell time? Prepare a **speech** about why telling time is important. 

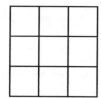

SYMMETRY
TIC-TAC-TOE MENU

Objectives Covered Through This Menu and These Activities
- Students will recognize and apply slides, turns, and flips.
- Students will recognize and create shapes that have symmetry.

Materials Needed by Students for Completion
- Mirrors
- Magazines (for collages)
- Tangram Template
- Poster board or large white paper

Time Frame
- 2–3 weeks—Students are given the menu as the unit is started. As the teacher presents lessons throughout the week, he or she should refer back to the menu options associated with that content. The teacher will go over all of the options for that content and have students place check marks in the boxes that represent the activities they are most interested in completing. As teaching continues over the next 2–3 weeks, activities chosen and completed should make a column or row. The teacher may choose to dedicate a learning center to working on menu products or simply allow time to work after other work is finished. When students complete this pattern, they will have completed one activity from each content area, learning style, or level of Bloom's Revised taxonomy, depending on the design of the menu.
- 1 week—At the start of the unit, the teacher chooses the three activities he or she feels are most valuable for students. Stations can be set up in the classroom. These three activities are available for student choice throughout the week as regular instruction takes place.
- 1–2 days—The teacher chooses an activity from the menu to use with the entire class.

Suggested Forms
- All-purpose rubric
- Free-choice proposal form if appropriate for content and level of students

Name:_____

SYMMETRY

Directions: Check the boxes you plan to complete. They should form a tic-tac-toe across or down. All activities must be completed by _____.

☐ **My Turn!** Create a **drawing** by taking one shape and turning it around a point. You can have more than one point that your shape turns around in your drawing. 	☐ **Am I Symmetrical?** Design a plan to see if your body is symmetrical. Use a measuring tape to complete your plan. Share your results on a **poster**. 	☐ **Don't Flip!** Make a set of tangrams out of cardboard using the Tangram Template. Create your own figures from the shapes and make a **brochure** that challenges your classmates to make your shapes.
☐ **Don't Flip!** Write a **skit** that shows how to tell if a drawing is a flip of the original. Use humor to help the audience remember! 	☐ **Free Choice On Turning** (Fill out your proposal form before beginning the free choice!) 	☐ **Am I Symmetrical?** Make a **collage** of symmetrical objects we see every day. Carefully draw the line of symmetry on each picture. 
☐ **Am I Symmetrical?** Create a **picture dictionary** for at least 10 items that are symmetrical. Include the line of symmetry on each picture with the definition of the object.	☐ **Don't Flip!** People often use mirrors to show flips. Choose a picture of your favorite animal, and use a mirror to draw the flip of the picture. Put the original picture next to your **drawing**. 	☐ **My Turn!** Write a **song or rap** that explains how to flip, turn, or slide a figure. 

Name:_____

TANGRAM TEMPLATE

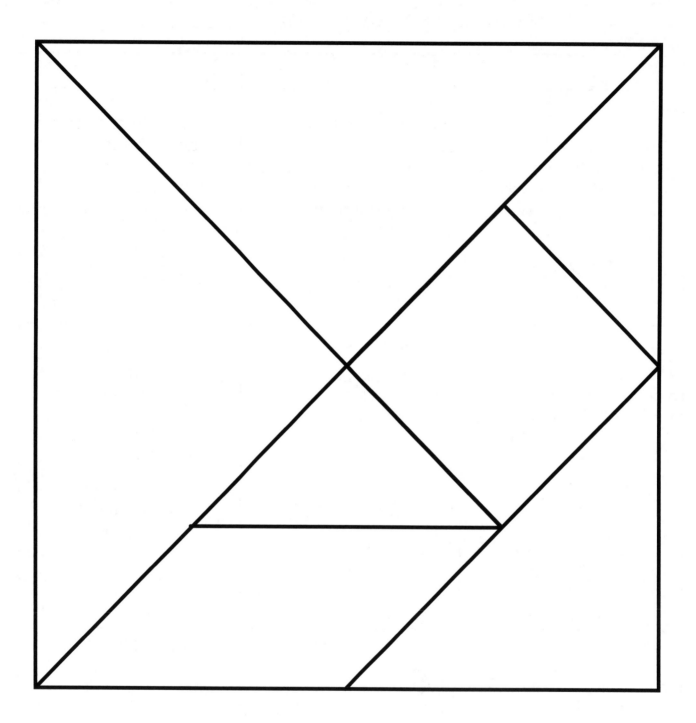

References

Anderson, L. W., & Krathwohl, D. R. (Eds.). (2001). *A taxonomy for learning, teaching, and assessing: A revision of Bloom's taxonomy of educational objectives.* New York, NY: Allyn & Bacon.

Keen, D. (2001). *Talent in the new millennium: Report on year one of the programme.* Retrieved from http://www.aare.edu.au/01pap/kee01007. htm

Magner, L. (2000). Reaching all children through differentiated assessment: The 2-5-8 plan. *Gifted Child Today, 23*(3), 48–50.

About the Author

After teaching science for more than 15 years, both overseas and in the U.S., **Laurie E. Westphal** now works as an independent gifted education and science consultant nationwide. She enjoys developing and presenting staff development on differentiation for various districts and conferences, working with teachers to assist them in planning and developing lessons to meet the needs of all students. Laurie currently resides in Houston, TX, and has made it her goal to convert as many teachers as she can to the differentiated lifestyle in the classroom and share her vision for real-world, product-based lessons that help all students become critical thinkers and effective problem solvers.

If you are interested in having Laurie speak at your next staff development day or conference, please visit her website, http://www. giftedconsultant.com, for additional information.

Common Core State Standards Alignment

This book aligns with an extensive number of the Common Core State Standards in Math. Please visit http://www.prufrock.com/ccss to download a complete packet of the standards that align with each individual menu in this book.

Additional Titles by the Author

Laurie E. Westphal has written many books on using differentiation strategies in the classroom, providing teachers of grades K–8 with creative, engaging, ready-to-use resources. Among them are:

Differentiating Instruction With Menus, Grades K–2
(Math, Language Arts, Science, and Social Studies volumes available)

Differentiating Instruction With Menus, Grades 3–5
(Math, Language Arts, Science, and Social Studies volumes available)

Differentiating Instruction With Menus, Grades 6–8
(Math, Language Arts, Science, and Social Studies volumes available)

Differentiating Instruction With Menus for the Inclusive Classroom, Grades K–2
(Math, Language Arts, Science, and Social Studies volumes available)

Differentiating Instruction With Menus for the Inclusive Classroom, Grades 3–5
(Math, Language Arts, Science, and Social Studies volumes available)

Differentiating Instruction With Menus for the Inclusive Classroom, Grades 6–8
(Math, Language Arts, Science, and Social Studies volumes available)

**For a current listing of Laurie's books, please visit
Prufrock Press at http://www.prufrock.com.**